A
HANDLIST OF
RHETORICAL
TERMS

A HANDLIST
OF RHETORICAL TERMS

A Guide for Students of English Literature

by Richard A. Lanham

UNIVERSITY OF CALIFORNIA PRESS
Berkeley and Los Angeles
1969

University of California Press
Berkeley and Los Angeles, California
Cambridge University Press
London, England
Copyright © 1968 by The Regents of the University of California

First Paper-bound Edition, 1969
Library of Congress Catalog Card Number: 68–31636
Designed by W. H. Snyder
Printed in the United States of America
SBN 520-01414-6

PREFACE

This is not an original rhetorical treatise. It is simply an attempt to put together in one convenient, accessible, inexpensive place the rhetorical terms that students of English literature, especially of the earlier periods, are likely to come across in their reading or to find useful in their writing. The terms are for the most part classical (though I have included Puttenham's Englished ones); they have been presented in a way aimed at the beginning student as well as the learned. The alphabetical list is designed for the reader who encounters an unfamiliar term, or one used in an unusual way, and needs a definition of it. The descriptive lists are designed for one who, having observed a particular verbal pattern in a text and helpless with an alphabetical list, seeks the proper name for it. Thus the alphabetical list tries to provide a manageable dictionary; the descriptive lists, something more like a thesaurus or synoptic grouping. I hope students of the classics may find this list useful, but it was not designed for them and so will not tell them, for example, whether *antimetabole* meant to Cicero precisely what it did to Rutulius Lupus. Neither does it attempt to decide which of several conflicting meanings for a term is to be preferred. There is a strong need for a careful survey of rhetorical terms, from the early Greeks through John Smith's *The Mysterie of Rhetorique Unvail'd*, with full-length articles on central, disputed forms and how their meanings change. But this is not it. In the face of continually surprising differences of opinion about what sometimes basic terms mean, I have merely listed the main differences. This should help. So should the reasonable attempt at cross-referencing. The final criterion for the *Handlist* as a whole has been ease of use, not any prescriptive system the compiler happens to favor. No attempt has been made to single out terms that any one rhetorical or critical body of opinion might favor, or think important. Such invidious distinctions, probably ill-advised, in practice become simply impossible: only the individual scholar can weight a term as he wishes.

In the best of all possible worlds, a list like this would canvass the whole of rhetorical theory. What I have done is use as a base the terms of the Renaissance theorists and add to them those terms that seem to me useful or common from Aristotle's *Rhetoric*, Demetrius' *On Style*, Quintilian, the various works by Cicero and the pseudo-Ciceronian *Rhetorica ad Herennium*, and Halm's *Rhetores Latini Minores* (which includes Bede's brief *Liber de Schematibus et Tropis*). I have also included all the terms in Susenbrotus' *Epitome Troporum ac Schematum* and Smith's *The Mysterie of Rhetorique Unvail'd*. The major modern secondary studies, from a glossary's point of view, are those by Sister Miriam Joseph, Warren Taylor, and Veré Rubel (see Works Cited), and I have used them continually, particularly for examples. I have also taken a few examples from Bartlett's *Familiar Quotations*. The best modern study of Greek rhetoric and rhetoricians is Kennedy's; his discussions, especially of Aristotle, have been invaluable. I know of no study of strictly Latin rhetoric to equal it. The Loeb Library *Rhetorica ad Herennium* has a useful chart-outline of figures in its introduction and a good index; Halm's index is very useful, as is Sister Miriam Joseph's (Halm's index is not fully cross-referenced). There is a convenient Index of Words at the end of the fourth volume of the Loeb Quintilian. The large Liddell and Scott *Lexicon*, and Lewis and Short's *A Latin Dictionary*, are essential, of course, especially for the less common terms. For logical terms I have mainly consulted Copi's *Introduction to Logic*. All references are to works listed in Works Cited. I have modernized spellings in the examples where appropriate, and identified them sufficiently to guide the occasional reader who will wish to seek out the context.

A work of this kind would perhaps most naturally fall into two categories, figures and other terms, and the reader deserves an explanation as to why it has not been followed here. It simply proved too difficult to decide, except on a prescriptive basis, what was a figure and what was not. (*See* TROPE.)

I have adopted the indications of syllable-stress found in *Webster's Third International* when it lists a term. For Latin terms not so listed as being in the language, I have generally followed the original stress. In a few instances, however, I have indicated a stress taken from an analogous word that *has* entered the language (e.g., "ge o GRAPH i a" rather than "ge o graph I a"). For stress of Greek terms, I have followed the Latin penultimate rule. An effort to prescribe pronunciation further than to indicate stress was given up as unnecessary and artificial.

I have not included all the possible variant spellings of terms, especially of Greek terms, as there are impossibly many. Thus *v* sometimes comes into English as "y", sometimes as "u"; the rough breathing is sometimes indicated by an "h" and sometimes not; Greek terminal "os" is sometimes Englished as "os", sometimes "us". Again, I have not tried to systematize an inconsistent usage.

The only guide I have followed in omitting terms has been my common sense, and its fallibility has been adequately demonstrated by the process. I have omitted quasi-rhetorical terms to be found in any handbook of literary terms, unless there was a special reason to include them. I have also omitted terms whose meanings are obvious and Latin equivalents for English terms (and vice versa): for example, *accentus* and accent. I have included a few common terms from logic for convenience. Synonyms are listed following the terms. I have omitted an etymology when it duplicates the definition. Since I have not included all the terms I have come across, it seems likely that I have not come across all the terms I might have wanted to include. Many of the terms listed are near synonyms and many have broad or disputed meanings. This should not deter anyone from using them with assurance; it certainly has not in the past.

Permission has been obtained for the reproduction of substantial quotations, as follows: Methuen & Co., Ltd. and Peter Smith for the material from J. W. Atkins' *English Literary Criticism: The Medieval Phase* which appears on pages 130–132; and W. W. Norton & Co., Inc. for the quotations and clock diagram from Graham Hough's *A Preface to the "Faerie Queene"* which appear on pages 4–5.

The efficient cause of the *Handlist* is evenly divided between a research grant from the University of California, Los Angeles, and the student who worked under it, Michael A. Anderegg. The earliest stimulus for such a list came to me from the teachings of the late Helge Kökeritz, the most recent, from the classical studies of my wife. *Gratias ago.*

R. A. L.

Los Angeles, California

Omnibus scriptores sua nomina dederunt,
sed varia et ut cuique fingenti placuit.

(QUINTILIAN)

CONTENTS

1. Alphabetical List of Terms   1

2. Terms Classified according to Divisions of Rhetoric   106
   2.1. Rhetoric: The five parts   106
   2.2. Rhetoric: The three branches   106
   2.3.1. Invention: Two kinds of proof, after
          Aristotle's *Rhetoric*   106
   2.3.2. Invention: Two types of logical proof   107
   2.3.3. Invention: Two kinds of topics, after
          Aristotle's *Rhetoric*   107
   2.3.4. Invention: Twenty-eight valid topics, after
          Aristotle's *Rhetoric*   107
   2.3.5. Invention: Ten invalid topics or fallacies of
          arguments, after Aristotle's *Rhetoric*   109
   2.3.6. Invention: Sixteen basic topics, after
          Cicero's *Topica*   110
   2.3.7. Invention: The commonplaces   110
   2.3.8. Invention: The main points at issue   111
   2.3.9. Invention: Thesis and hypothesis (general
          and particular arguments), after Hermagoras   111
   2.4. Arrangement: The seven parts of an oration   112
   2.5.1. Style: The three types   113
   2.5.2. Style: The four virtues   115
   2.5.3. Style: The figures   116

3. The Terms by Type   117
   3.1. Addition, Subtraction, and Substitution of
        Letters and Syllables   117

3.2. Addition, Subtraction, and Substitution of
Words, Phrases, and Clauses   117
3.3. Amplification   118
3.4. Balance, Antithesis, and Paradox   119
3.5. Brevity   120
3.6. Description   120
3.7. Emotional Appeals and Exhortations   121
3.8. Example, Allusion, and Citation of Authority   122
3.9. Metaphorical Substitutions and Puns   123
3.10. Repetitive Patterns   124
3.10.1. Repetition of letters, syllables, and sounds 124
3.10.2. Repetition of words   124
3.10.3. Repetition of clauses, phrases, and ideas   125
3.11. Techniques of Argument   125
3.12. Ungrammatical, Illogical, or Unusual Uses
of Language   128

4. Terms Classified as Ornaments   130
    4.1. Difficult Ornaments: Ten basic tropes   130
    4.2. Easy Ornaments   130
    4.2.1. Figures of words   130
    4.2.2. Figures of thought   132

5. Terms Especially Useful in Literary Criticism   133

6. Some Important Dates   144

7. Works Cited   146

1.

ALPHABETICAL LIST OF TERMS

Abbaser. Puttenham's term for **Tapinosis.**

Ablatio (a BLA ti o; L. "taking away") — **Aphaeresis.**

Abode. Puttenham's term for **Commoratio.**

Abominatio (a bom i NA ti o; L. "deserving imprecation or abhorrence") — **Bdelygma.**

Abscissio (ab SCISS i o; L. "breaking off") — **Apocope.**

Abuse. Puttenham's term for **Catachresis.**

Abusio (a BUS i o; L. "harsh use of tropes") — **Catachresis.**

Acclamatio (ac cla MA ti o; L. "calling to, exclamation, shout") — **Epiphonema.**

Accumulatio (ac cum u LA ti o; L. "heaping up") — **Synathroesmus; Congeries.** Heaping up praise or accusation to emphasize or summarize points or inferences already made:

> "He [the defendant] is the betrayer of his own self-respect, and the waylayer of the self-respect of others; covetous, intemperate, irascible, arrogant; disloyal to his parents, ungrateful to his friends . . ." (*Rhetorica ad Herennium*, IV, xl, 52).

Accusatio (ac cu SA ti o; L. "complaint, accusation, indictment") — **Categoria.**

Accusatio Concertativa (ac cu SA tl o con cer ta TI va; L. "recrimination, countercharge") — **Anticategoria.**

Actio (AC ti o). The Latin term for Delivery, the fifth of the five parts of rhetoric.

Acyrologia (a cy ro LO gi a; G. "incorrect in phraseology") — **Acyron; Improprietas; Uncouthe.** Use of an inexact or illogical word; malapropism; for Quintilian, impropriety. "O villain! thou wilt be condemn'd into everlasting redemption for this" (*Much Ado About Nothing*, IV, ii).

Adage (L. "proverb") — **Proverb,** *q.v. Also* **Gnome; Maxim; Sententia; Aphorismus.** *See also* **Paroemia.**

Addubitation (L. "doubting") — **Aporia.**

Adfictio (ad FIC ti o; L. "invent, add by invention") — **Paronomasia.**

Adhortatio (ad hor TA ti o; L. "exhortation, encouragement") — **Protrope.**

Adianoeta (a di a no ET a; G. "unintelligible"). An expression that has an obvious meaning and an unsuspected secret one beneath. So one says to a good friend who is also a poor novelist: "I will lose no time in reading your new book." Or, as the Foundation says to the unsuccessful applicant: "For your work, we have nothing but praise."

Adinventio (ad in VEN ti o; L. "invention") — **Pareuresis.**

Adjudicatio (ad ju di CA ti o; L. "adjudication") — **Epicrisis.**

Adjunctio (ad JUNC ti o; L. "joining to"). The use of one verb to express two similar ideas at the beginning or end of successive clauses. Sometimes **Zeugma.** *See also* **Symploce:**

>"Fades physical beauty with disease or age," *or*

>"Either with disease or age physical beauty fades."

>(*Rhetorica ad Herennium*, IV, xxvii, 38)

Admiratio (ad mir A ti o) — **Thaumasmus.**

Admittance. Puttenham's term for **Paramologia.**

Admonitio (ad mo NI ti o; L. "reminding, recalling to mind, suggestion") — **Paraenesis.**

Adnexio (ad NEX i o; L. "binding to") — **Zeugma.**

Adnominatio (ad no mi NA ti o); alt. sp. **Agnominatio.**

Adtenuata (ad ten u A ta; L. "weakened, reduced"). The third, or simple, type of style.

Adynata (a DY na ta) — **Adynaton; Impossibilia.** A stringing together of impossibilities. Sometimes, a confession that words fail us.

Aenigma; alt. sp. **Enigma.**

Aenos (AE nos; G. "tale, story [esp. with a moral], fable"). The quoting of wise sayings from fables.

Aetiologia (ae ti o LO gi a; G. "giving a cause"); alt. sp. **Etiologia — Redditio Causae; Reason Rend; Tell Cause; Enthymeme.** Giving a cause or reason; enthymeme (abridged syllogism), since by giving first a cause and then a result, an inverted abbreviated syllogism is sometimes created, as in Hamlet on the players: "Let them be well us'd; for they are the abstract and brief chronicles of the time" (II, ii).

Affirming the Consequent (Fallacy of). To affirm the second part (consequent) of a hypothetical proposition rather than the first:

If John ran a four-minute mile he is a fast miler.
John is a fast miler.
Therefore, John has run a four-minute mile.
Opposite of **Denying the Antecedent.**
Aganactesis (a ga nac TE sis; G. "vexation") — **Indignatio.**
Aggressio (ag GRES si o; L. "going forward"; rhet. "a rhetorical syllogism") — **Epicheireme.**
Agnominatio (ag no mi NA ti o; L. "two words of different meaning but similar sound brought together"); alt. sp. **Adnominatio** — **Paronomasia.** A distinction sometimes has been made, however, between agnominatio as mainly a play on sounds of words, paranomasia as a play on sense of words.
Aischrologia (ais chro LOG i a; G. "foul language, abuse"); alt. sp. **Aschrologia** — **Cacemphaton.**
Allegorical Level. *See* **Allegory.**
Allegory (G. "speaking otherwise than one seems to speak") — **Inversio; False Semblant.**
1. Extending a metaphor through an entire speech or passage; the rhetorical meaning is narrower than the literary one, though congruent with it: the allegory is sometimes called "pure" when every main term in the passage has a double significance, "mixed" when one or more terms do not.
2. One of four levels or senses of interpretation common in medieval and Renaissance exegesis. Allegorizing of this sort had begun with Greek commentary on Homer and by the Middle Ages was common in reading Virgil as well: (*a*) Literal; (*b*) Allegorical; (*c*) Moral or Tropological; (*d*) Anagogical or Spiritual. Or, as the medieval catchverse has it:
    Littera gesta docet,
    Quid credas, allegoria
    Moralia, quid agas,
    Quo tendas, anagogia.
One of these two definitions ought to satisfy most rhetorical uses of the term. As used in literary criticism, however, the term is so complex as to lie well outside the scope of such a listing as this. For an inadequate suggestion of how the term moves over into rhetorical analysis of literature, perhaps brief quotations from two recent authorities may be of some help. Of the range of literature that can be called allegorical, Angus Fletcher writes:
    "An allegorical mode of expression characterizes a quite extraordinary variety of literary kinds: chivalric

or picaresque romances and their modern equivalent, the 'western,' utopian political satires, quasi-philo-sophical anatomies, personal attacks in epigrammatic form, pastorals of all sorts, apocalyptic visions, ency-clopedic epics . . . naturalistic muck-raking novels whose aim is to propagandize social change, imaginary voyages . . . detective stories . . . fairy tales . . . debate poems . . . complaints like Alain de Lille's *De Planctu Naturae* and Allen Ginsberg's 'Howl'. . . ."
(*Allegory: The Theory of a Symbolic Mode*, pp. 3–4)
The problem here would seem to be a conception of allegory so wide as to equal all "meaning" in literature. (Northrop Frye has made the analogous point [*Anatomy of Criticism*, pp. 89 ff.] that all commentary on literature is allegorical, changing one kind of meaning into another.) Among the descriptions of the range of *meaning* the term "allegory" covers (rather than the range of *works* to which it can apply), Graham Hough's is perhaps the clearest. In an analysis that builds on Frye's in the *Anatomy*, he uses the clock diagram that appears below.

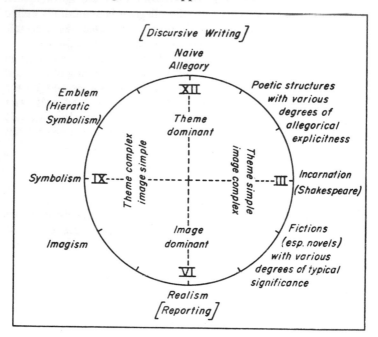

He explains it this way:

"At twelve o'clock we have naive allegory. . . . In naive allegory theme is completely dominant, image merely a rhetorical convenience with no life of its own. . . . It is properly described in the terms which anti-allegorical critics use of allegory in general — a picture-writing to transcribe preconceived ideas.

"At three o'clock we have the kind of literature best represented by the work of Shakespeare, in which theme and image are completely fused and the relation between them is only implicit, never open or enforced. We have not yet found a name for this. . . . I shall call it incarnation. . . .

"At six o'clock, opposed to naive allegory, we find what I have called realism. Here image is predominant and theme at a minimum. That literature which presents itself as the direct mimesis of common experience comes here — realist and quasi-documentary fiction, descriptive writing, and so forth.

"At nine o'clock we find symbolism, like incarnation a form in which theme and image have equal weight, but opposed to incarnation because the relation between the two elements is different. In symbolism there is none of the harmonious wholeness of incarnational literature. Theme and image are equally present, they assert their unity, but the unity is never achieved, or if it is, it is only a unity of tension.

". . . with symbolism we enter the last quarter and are already well on our way back to naive allegory again. But as before there is an intermediate stage. Halfway between symbolism and naive allegory we have what I will call emblem or hieratic symbolism. It exists largely outside literature — its special field is iconography and religious imagery. There is a tendency for symbolism to become fixed; the image shrinks and becomes stereotyped, and theme expands. . . . And so by a commodious vicus of recirculation we come back to our starting point."

(*A Preface to "The Faerie Queene,"* pp. 106 ff.)

Alleotheta (all eo THETA). Substitution of one case, gender, number, tense, or mood for another. **Anthimeria; Antiptosis; Enal-**

lage; **Hendiadys** are sometimes subdivisions of this term, sometimes synonyms; examples are listed under them.

Alliteration. Originally, recurrence of an initial consonant sound (and so a type of **Consonance,** *q.v.*), but now sometimes used of vowel sounds as well (where it overlaps with **Assonance,** *q.v.*):

> "Warm-laid grave of a womb-life grey;
> Manger, maiden's knee. . . ."
>
> (G. M. Hopkins)

Recurrence of both kinds of alliteration at once (ark, art, arm) would yield what is sometimes called "front rhyme." **Alliteration** is an early modern term; more common before was **Paroemion.**

Alloiosis (al loi o sis; G. "difference, alteration"). Breaking down a subject into alternatives: In youth we seek either glory or money. If used on a narrow scale, this becomes **Antithesis** (Quintilian IX, iii, 81). On a large scale, he continues, it is no figure. It may also mean **Hypallage** (2), that is, **Metonymy** (VIII, vi, 23).

Amara Irrisio (a MAR a   ir RIS i o; L. "bitter laughing at") — **Sarcasmus.**

Ambage. Puttenham's term for **Periphrasis.**

Ambiguous. Puttenham's term for **Amphibologia.**

Ambitus (AM bi tus) — **Period.**

Amphibologia (am phi bo LOG i a; G. "ambiguity") — **Ambiguous.** Ambivalence of grammatical structure, usually by mispunctuation; produces misconception:

> "Cassio: Dost thou hear, my honest friend?
> Clown: No, I hear not your honest friend; I hear you."
>
> (*Othello*, III, i)

Amphidiorthosis (am phi di or THO sis). To hedge a charge made in anger by qualifying it either before the charge has been made or (sometimes repeating the charge in other words) after.

Amplificatio (am pli fi CA ti o; L. "enlargement") — **Confirmation.** The Latin term for the fifth part of a seven-part oration.

Amplification. Rhetorical device used to expand a simple statement; one sixteenth-century English theorist isolated five means of amplification (comparison, division, accumulation, intimation, progression) and the following figures that amplify: **Hyperbole; Correctio; Paralepsis; Accumulatio; Divisio; Interrogatio; Exclamatio; Synoeciosis; Antithesis; Sententia.** Another theorist lists seventeen figures, a third sixty-four; logically, *any* figure except those specifically aimed at brevity should fit.

Anacephalaeosis (ana cepha LAE osis; G. "summary") — **Enumeratio** (2). *See also* **Anamnesis.**

Anachinosis — **Anacoenosis.**

Anaclasis (a NAC la sis; G. "bending back") — **Antanaclasis.**

Anacoenosis (a na coe NO sis; G. "communicate with, take counsel with") — **Anachinosis; Impartener.** *See also* **Epitrope; Apostrophe.** Asking the opinion of one's readers or hearers. Smith (*Mysterie of Rhetorique*) adds that this figure is elegantly used with such as are (1) dead, (2) the judge, (3) absent, (4) inanimate. An example of this last:

> "Then ev'n of fellowship, ô Moone, tell me
> Is constant *Love* deem'd there but want of wit?
> Are Beauties there as proud as here they be?
> Do they above love to be lov'd, and yet
> Those Lovers scorne whom that *Love* doth possesse?
> Do they call *Vertue* there ungratefulnesse?"
> (Sidney, *Astrophil and Stella*, XXXI)

Anacoluthon (a na co LU thon; G. "inconsistent, anomalous") — **Anantapodoton.** Ending a sentence with a different structure from that with which it began. Both a vice and a device to demonstrate emotion:

> "Rather proclaim it, Westmoreland, through my host,
> That he which hath no stomach to this fight,
> Let him depart."
> (*Henry V*, IV, iii)

Anadiplosis (a na di PLO sis; G. "doubled back") — **Gradatio; Palilogia** (1); **Reduplicatio; Duplicatio; Redouble.** *See also* **Conduplicatio.** Repetition of the last word of one line or clause to begin the next:

> "For I have loved long, I crave reward
> Reward me not unkindly: think on kindness,
> Kindness becommeth those of high regard
> Regard with clemency a poor man's blindness. . . ."
> (Bartholomew Griffin, *Fidessa*, XVI)

Anagogical Level. *See* **Allegory.**

Analogy (G. "equality of ratios, proportion") — **Proportio.** *See also* **Simile.** Reasoning or arguing from parallel cases.

Anamnesis (a nam NE sis; G. "remembrance") — **Recordatio.** *See also* **Enumeratio.** Recalling matters of the past; ideas, events, persons:

"By the waters of Babylon, there we sat down, yea, we wept,
When we remembered Zion."

(Psalm 137)

Anangeon — Dicaeologia.

Anantapodoton (a nant a PO do ton; G. "without apodosis; hypothetical proposition wanting the consequent clause") — **Anacoluthon.**

Anaphora (a NAPH ora; G. "carrying back") — **Repetitio; Iteratio; Epanaphora; Epembasis; Report.** Repetition of the same word at the beginning of successive clauses or verses:

"To think on death it is a misery, To think on life it is a
vanity; To think on the world verily it is, To think that
here man hath no perfect bliss."

(Puttenham)

Anapodoton (a na PO do ton; G. "not given back"). Omitting a main clause from a conditional sentence: "If you do as I have counseled you, and be ruled by your friends, they will do for you, if not, well, I will say no more" (Peacham).

Anastrophe (a NAS tro phe; G. "turning back") — **Perversio; Reversio.** *See also* **Hysteron Proteron.**

1. Kind of **Hyperbaton:** unusual arrangement of words or clauses within a sentence.

"Yet I'll not shed her blood;
Nor scar that whiter skin of hers than snow."

(*Othello*, V, ii)

Quintilian would confine anastrophe to a transposition of two words only.

2. **Anadiplosis.**

Anatomy (G. "cutting up, dissection"). The analysis of an issue into its constituent parts, for ease of discussion or clarity of exegesis; the term is not a traditional one, but has been increasingly used as a generic term for a technique that includes a number of the traditional dividing and particularizing figures.

Anemographia (a nem o GRAPH i a). Description of the wind. *See also* **Prosopographia; Topographia; Chorographia; Chronographia; Geographia; Hydrographia; Dendrographia.**

Anoiconometon (a noi con o ME ton; G. "not set in order"). ". . . when there is no good disposition of the words, but all are confused up and down and set without order" (Sherry). Want of proper arrangement.

Antanaclasis (an tan AC la sis; G. "reflection, bending back") —

Transplacement; Anaclasis; Rebounde; Reciprocatio; Refractio.
1. Homonymic pun: "My forces razde, thy banners raisd within" (Sidney, *Astrophil and Stella*, XXXVI).
2. Sometimes **Ploce.**

Antanagoge (an ta na GO ge; G. "leading or bringing up against; instead") — **Compensatio** (2); **Recompencer.** Ameliorating a fault or difficulty implicitly admitted by balancing an unfavorable aspect with a favorable one:

> "I must needs say, that my wife is a shrew,
> But such a huswife as I know but a few."
> (Puttenham)

Antapodosis (an ta PO do sis; G. "giving back in return") — **Redditio Contraria.** A simile in which the objects compared correspond in several respects:

> "As they say that those, among the Greek musicians,
> who cannot become players on the lyre, may become
> players on the flute, so we see that those who cannot
> become orators betake themselves to the study of law."
> (Cicero, *Pro Murena*)

Antenantiosis (an te nan ti o sis; G. "positive statement made in a negative form") — **Litotes.**

Ante Occupatio (an te oc cu PA ti o) — **Procatalepsis.**

Anthimeria (an thi MER i a; G ."one part for another"). Functional shift, using one part of speech for another: "His complexion is perfect gallows" (*Tempest*, I, i). *See also* **Enallage; Alleotheta.**

Anthypallage (an thy PAL la ge; G. "substitution"). Change of grammatical case for emphasis.

Anthypophora (an thy PO pho ra; G. "reply").
1. **Hypophora; Responce.**
2. Replying to anticipated objections:

> "If there be any in this assembly, any dear friend
> of Caesar's, to him I say, that Brutus' love to
> Caesar was no less than his. If then that friend
> demand why Brutus rose against Caesar, this is
> my answer: — Not that I loved Caesar less, but
> that I loved Rome more."
> (*Julius Caesar*, III, ii)

Anticategoria (an ti cat e GOR i a) — **Accusatio Concertativa.** Mutual accusation or recrimination.

Anticiceronianism. The revolt against a slavish imitation of Cicero's periodic prose style. Morris Croll saw three basic anti-Ciceronian tendencies:

1. The curt Senecan style (Lipsius).
2. The loose Senecan style (Montaigne).
3. The obscure (Bacon).

See also **Ciceronian Style; Period; Senecan Style.**

Anticipatio (an ti ci PAT i o; L. "preconception") — **Procatalepsis.**

Antimetabole (an ti me TAB o le; G. "turning about") — **Chiasmus; Commutatio; Permutatio; Counterchange.** In English, inverting the order of repeated words to sharpen their sense or to contrast the ideas they convey or both (AB:BA); chiasmus and commutatio sometimes imply a more precise balance and reversal, antimetabole a looser, but they are virtual synonyms: "I pretty, and my saying apt? or I apt, and my saying pretty?" (*Love's Labour's Lost*, I, ii).

Latin use of the term was slightly different from the English and not precisely synonymous with chiasmus. Quintilian, for example, defines it:

> "Antithesis may also be effected by employing that *figure,* known as [antimetabole], by which words are repeated in different cases, tenses, moods, etc., as for instance when we say, *non ut edam vivo, sed ut vivam, edo* [I do not live to eat, but eat to live]" (IX, iii, 85).

Antinomy (an TIN o my; G. lit. "opposition of law; ambiguity in law"). A comparison of one law to another, or of one part of a law to another.

Antiphora (an TIPH or a; G. "contrary motion") — **Anthypophora.**

Antiphrasis (an TIPH ra sis; G. "expression by the opposite") — **Broad Floute.** Irony of one word, calling a "dwarf" a "giant," an "enemy" a "friend."

Antiptosis (an tip TO sis; G. lit. "exchange of case") — **Casu Pro Casu.** Substituting one case for another as the accusative for the dative; a type of **Alleotheta.** "I give you this gift" *for* "I give this gift to you;" "he is condemned for murder" *for* "he is condemned of murder" (Peacham).

See also **Enallage.**

Antirrhesis (an tir RHE sis; G. "refutation, counterstatement"). Rejecting an argument because of its insignificance, error, or wickedness:

"Then said his wife unto him, Dost thou still retain thine integrity? curse God and die.

"But he said unto her, Thou speakest as one of the foolish women speaketh. What? shall we receive good at the hand of God, and shall we not receive evil?"

(Job 2:9–10)

Antisagoge (an tis a GO ge) — **Compensatio** (1).

1. Contrasting evaluations; rewarding the virtuous, punishing the vicious. Leontes, in *Winter's Tale*, says:

"Do't, and thou hast the one half of my heart;
Do't not, thou splitt'st thine own."

(I, ii)

2. Stating first one side of a proposition, then the other, with equal vigor:

"Love seeketh not Itself to please,
Nor for itself hath any care,
But for another gives its ease,
And builds a Heaven in Hell's despair."

"Love seeketh only Self to please,
To bind another to Its delight,
Joys in another's loss of ease,
And builds a Hell in Heaven's despite."

(Blake, "The Clod and the Pebble")

Antistasis (an TI sta sis; G. "opposition, counterplea") — **Contentio.** Repetition of a word in a different or contrary sense: "I wasted time and now doth time waste me" (*Richard II*, V, v).

Antisthecon (an TIS the con) — **Transposition; Metathesis.** A type of **Metaplasm:** substituting one letter or sound for another within a word: "strond" for "strand."

Antistrephon (an TIS tre phon; G. "to turn to the opposite side"). An argument that turns one's opponent's arguments or proofs to one's own purpose.

Antistrophe (an TIS tro phe; G. "turning about").

1. **Conversio; Conversum; Counterturne; Epiphora; Epistrophe** (1). Repetition of a closing word or words at the end of several successive clauses, sentences, or verses:

"Where affections bear rule, there reason is subdued, honesty is subdued, good will is subdued, and all things else that withstand evil, for ever are subdued."

(Wilson)

2. The repetition of a word or phrase in a second context in the same position it held in an earlier and similar context:

". . . anon with great disdain,
She shuns my love, and after by a train
She seeks my love, and saith she loves me most,
But seeing her love, so lightly won and lost." etc.

(Peacham)

Antithesis (an TITH e sis; G. "opposition") — **Antitheton; Contentio; Contraposition; Oppositio.** *See also* **Syncrisis.** Conjoining contrasting ideas, as in Sidney's *Arcadia*:

". . . neither the one hurt her, nor the other help her;
just without partiality, mighty without contradiction,
liberal without losing, wise without curiosity. . . ."

Antitheton (an TITH e ton; G. "opposed") — **Antithesis; Quarreller.**

Antonomasia (an ton o MA si a; G. "to name instead," "to use an epithet, patronymic, instead of a proper name") — **Pronominatio; Nominatio; Surnamer.** Descriptive phrase for proper name or proper name for quality associated with it: "If someone speaking of the Gracchi should say: 'Surely the grandsons of Africanus did not behave like this' " (*Rhetorica ad Herennium*, IV, xxxi, 42).

Quintilian points out the similarity to **Synecdoche.**

Apaetesis (a pae TE sis). A matter put aside in anger is resumed later.

Aphaeresis (a PHAER e sis; G. "taking away") — **Ablatio.** Omitting a syllable from the beginning of a word: "what 'cerns it you." The converse (omission of final vowel) is elision.

Aphelia (a PHE li a; G. "plainness"). Plainness of writing or speech.

Aphorismus (a phor IS mus; G. "distinction, definition") — **Proverb,** *q.v.*

1. *Also* **Apothegm; Maxim; Gnome; Sententia; Adage.** *See also* **Paroemia.**

2. A point is made or a description amplified by questioning the force or applicability of a word or an aphorism:

"What laws be these, if at least wise they may be
termed laws, which bear in them so vile customs,
and not rather firebrands of the city, and the
plague of the whole commonweal."

(Day)

3. **Correctio.**
Apocarteresis (a po car ter E sis) — **Tolerantia.** Giving up one
hope and turning to another: No man can help me; I'll pray.
Peacham uses the term, having borrowed it, presumably, from
Quintilian, VIII, v, 23, where the word is used, in Greek, in its
usual meaning: "to kill oneself by fasting," i.e. to give up all
hope. Quintilian's context does not altogether support Peacham's
redefinition.
Apocope (a POC o pe; G. "cutting off") — **Abscissio.** *See also*
Aposiopesis (1). Omitting the last syllable or letter of a word:
"As seld I have the chance" (*Troilus and Cressida*, IV, v).
Apocrisis (a POC ri sis; G. "answer") — **Hypophora.**
Apodioxis (a po di ox is; G. "driving away") — **Rejectio.** Reject-
ing an argument indignantly as impertinent or absurdly false.
See also **Antirrhesis; Diasyrmus.**

> "But he turned, and said unto Peter, Get thee behind
> me, Satan: thou art an offence unto me: for thou sa-
> vourest not the things that be of God, but those that
> be of men."

(Matt. 16:23)

Apodixis (a po DIX is; G. "of the nature of demonstration"); alt.
sp. **Apodeixis — Experientia.** *See also* **Antirrhesis.**
1. Confirming a statement by reference to generally accepted
   principles or experience:
   > "Be not deceived; God is not mocked: for whatso-
   > ever a man soweth, that shall he also reap."

   (Gal. 6:7)
2. An incomplete **Epicheireme;** the proof of an epicheireme.
   Quintilian summarizes classical agreement, or disagreement,
   with the definition: "a method of proving what is not certain by means of what is certain" (V, x, 8). He does not
   give an example, however. He does remark that "some
   think that an *apodeixis* is a portion of an *epicheireme*,
   namely the part containing the proof." This would seem to
   agree with Aristotle:
   > "The enthymeme must consist of a few proposi-
   > tions, fewer often than those which make up the
   > normal syllogism. For if any of these propositions
   > is a familiar fact, there is no need even to mention
   > it; the hearer adds it himself. Thus, to show that

Dorieus has been victor in a contest for which the
prize is a crown, it is enough to say 'for he has
been victor in the Olympic games,' without adding
'And in the Olympic games the prize is a crown,'
a fact which everybody knows."

(*Rhetorica*, I, 1357ª)

Apologue (AP o logue; G. "account, story, fable") — **Fable.**

Apomnemonysis (a po mne mo NY sis; G. "recounting, summarizing") — **Commemoratio.** The quotation of an approved authority from memory:

"Ye hypocrites, well did Esaias prophesy of you, saying,
This people draweth nigh unto me with their mouth,
and honoureth me with their lips; but their heart is
far from me."

(Matt. 15:7–8)

Apophasis (a POPH a sis; G. "denial").

1. **Expeditio.** All alternatives rejected except one.
"It must needs be that this controversy touching
the sacrament must stand either upon the much
pressing and rigour of the words, or upon the
meaning and understanding of them. The words as
they stand bring with them great inconveniences,
to wit, to expositors, and the other texts. The
meaning doth not so, but avoideth all these inconveniences & satisfieth reason, expositors, &
texts of the scripture: wherefore wit, expositor &
scripture thinketh it better to take the sentence,
than the word."

(Sherry)

2. Pretending to deny what is really affirmed.
3. Giving many reasons and confuting each one.

Apophonema (a po pho NE ma; G. "denial" plus G. "decision, judgment"?). A **Sententia** put in antithetical form: "The roots of literature are harsh; its fruits, delightful."

Apoplanesis (a po pla NE sis; G. "digression"). Evading the issue by digressing:

"JUSTICE: Sir John, I sent for you before your expedition to Shrewsbury.

FALSTAFF: An't please your lordship, I hear his Majesty is return'd with some discomfort from Wales.

> JUSTICE: I talk not of his Majesty: you would not
> come when I sent for you.
> FALSTAFF: And I hear, moreover, his Highness is fall'n
> into this same whoreson apoplexy."
>> (*II Henry IV*, I, ii)

Aporia (a por I a; G. "difficulty, being at a loss") — **Dubitatio; Addubitation; Diaporesis; Doubtfull.** True or feigned doubt or deliberation about an issue. Peacham cites Cicero: "whether he took them from his fellows more impudently, gave them to a harlot more lasciviously, removed them from the Roman people more wickedly, or altered them more presumptuously, I cannot well declare."

Aposiopesis (ap o si o PE sis; G. "becoming silent") — **Praecisio; Reticentia; Obticentia; Silence; Interruption; Interpellatio.**

1. Stopping suddenly in midcourse — leaving a statement unfinished:
> "He said you were, I dare not tell you plain:
> For words once out, never return again."
>> (Puttenham)

2. An idea, though unexpressed, is clearly perceived: as when Sir Winston Churchill is said to have replied to an impertinent question, "The answer to your question, sir, is in the plural, and they bounce."

Apostrophe (G. "turning away") — **Aversio; Turne Tale.** *See also* **Ecphonesis.** Breaking off discourse to address directly some person or thing either present or absent:
> "Soul of the age!
> The applause, delight, the wonder of our stage!
> My Shakespeare rise!"
>> (Ben Jonson)

Apothegm (AP o thegm; G. "terse saying") — **Proverb,** *q.v. Also* **Gnome; Maxim; Sententia; Aphorismus; Adage.** A short, pithy statement of a general truth. *See also* **Paroemia.**

Applicatio (ap pli CA ti o; L. "joining oneself to") — **Refutation.**

Appositio (ap po SIT i o; L. "a setting before") — **Epergesis.**

Ara (A ra; G. "prayer, vow, curse") — **Execratio; Imprecatio.** Curse or imprecation, especially at length:
> "Let his days be few;
>   and let another take his office.
> Let his children be fatherless,
>   And his wife a widow.

Let his children be vagabonds, and beg:
And let them seek their bread out of their desolate places."
(Psalm 109:8–10)

Argument. *See* **Proof; Topics.**

Argumentum ad Baculum (ar gu MEN tum   ad   BAC u lum; L. "scepter, staff"). *See* **Fallacy.** An appeal to force (literally, "to the staff, or club") to settle the question.

Argumentum ad Hominem (HO min em; L. "man"). *See* **Fallacy.**
  1. Abuse of your opponent's character.
  2. Basing your argument on what you know of your opponent's character.

Churchill's reputed description of Atlee may exemplify both: "He was a modest man, with much to be modest about."

Argumentum ad Ignorantiam (ig no RANT iam). *See* **Fallacy.** A proposition is true if it has not been proved false.

Argumentum ad Misericordiam (mi se ri COR di am). *See* **Fallacy.** Appeal to the mercy of the hearers.

Argumentum ad Populum (POP u lum). *See* **Fallacy.** An appeal to the crowd.

Argumentum ad Verecundiam (ver e CUN di am). *See* **Fallacy.** An appeal to reverence for authority, to accepted traditional values.

Argumentum ex Concessis (con CES sis). *See* **Fallacy.** Reasoning that the conclusion of an argument is sound, on the basis of the truth of the premises of one's opponent. He might have exaggerated the soundness of his premise for *his* purposes. You use the exaggeration for yours.

Ariphmon (a RIPH mon; perhaps G. arithmon, "quantity, mere number, as opposed to quality"). ". . . a kind of endighting drawn out along, utterly void of all sweet and round composition" (Sherry).

Arrangement — Dispositio; Taxis (1). The second of the five traditional parts of rhetoric, that having to do with the ordering of arguments.

Ars Dictaminis (dic TA min is; L. "art of expressing in language, drawing up a document") **— Dictamen.** That branch of medieval rhetorical theory which laid down the rules for the composition of legal, or formal state, documents. Both poetry and prose were in its province. Eric Auerbach has described its principal stylistic elements in this way: "rhythmical movement of clauses, rhymed prose, sound patterns and figures of speech, unusual vocabulary, complex and pompous sentence structure" (*Literary Language and Its Public*, p. 273). Its three conventional subdivisions were: metrical, rhythmical, prose. The training for and practice of *ars dictaminis* gradually came to usurp much of the doctrine formerly grouped under *ars rhetorica*. This latter increasingly came to mean only the study of figures, or ornaments.

Ars Praedicandi (prae di CAN di). The part of medieval rhetorical theory concerned with eloquence in preaching.

Articulo (ar TI cu lo; L. "to divide in single parts"); alt. sp. **Articulus — Asyndeton.**

Artificial Proofs. Proofs extracted by the orator from his cause; the interpretation the orator can put on the "inartificial" proofs or evidence; properly speaking not "proofs" at all. *See* **Proof.**

Ascendus (as CEN dus; L. "ascent, climb") — **Climax.**

Aschematiston (a sche ma TIS ton) — **Aschematon; Male Figuratum.**

1. Absence of ornamental or figured language: a perfectly plain, normal style.
2. Unskillful use of figures.

The two terms are used interchangeably for the two meanings.

Asiatismus (a si a TIS mus). ". . . a kind of endighting used of the Asians, full of figures, and words, lacking matter" (Sherry). Asiatic Manner: highly ornamented style common when the polyracial populations of Asia wrote in Greek without the restraints traditional in earlier stylistic decorum. Cicero (*Brutus*, 325) distinguishes two types of Asianism: the "subtle-sententious" and the "grandiloquent-impetuous"; in practice, modern scholars may have difficulty distinguishing the two. *See* **Atticism; Rhodian Style.**

Asphalia (as pha LI a; G. "security, certainty, bond") — **Securitas; Certitudo.**

1. Offering oneself as surety for a bond:
   "ANTONIO: I dare be bound again.

   My soul upon the forfeit. . . ."
   (*Merchant of Venice*, V, i)
2. Assuring someone of something:
   "Judah, thou art he whom thy brethren shall praise: thy hand shall be in the neck of thine enemies; thy father's children shall bow down before thee."

   (Gen. 49:8)

Assonance (L. "to sound to"). Resemblance or similarity in sound between vowel-sounds preceded and followed by differing consonant-sounds in words in proximity: will; hinder; nit. *See also* **Alliteration; Paronomasia.**

Asteismus (a ste IS mus; G. "refined, witty talk") — **Civill Jest; Merry Scoffe; Urbanitas.** Facetious or mocking answer that plays on a word:

"LONGAVILLE: I desire her name.
 BOYET: She hath but one for herself; to desire that were
  a shame.
 LONGAVILLE: Pray you, sir, whose daughter?
 BOYET: Her mother's I have heard."
             (*Love's Labour's Lost*, II, i)

Asyndeton (a SYN de ton; G. "unconnected") — **Articulo; Brachylogia; Dialyton** (1); **Dissolutio; Loose Language; Dialelumenon.** Omission of conjunctions between words, phrases, or clauses:
 "Faynt, wearie, sore, emboyled, grieved, brent
 With heat, toyle, wounds, armes, smart, and inward fire."
             (Spenser, *Faerie Queene*, I, xi, 28)
Opposite of **Polysyndeton.**

Atticism. The mid-first-century B.C. reaction against Asianism (**Asiatismus,** *q.v.*) called itself "Atticism" because it went back for a model to the Attic orators of the classical period. The word, applied to the styles of other literatures, has generally meant a style that is the opposite of the ornamental, one brief, witty, sometimes epigrammatic. *See* **Rhodian Style.** (For further clarification, see Croll, *Style, Rhetoric, and Rhythm.*)

Attribution. Puttenham's term for **Epitheton.**

Augendi Causa (au GEN di CAU sa; L. "for the purpose of increasing"). Raising the voice for emphasis.

Auxesis (aux ES is; G. "increase, amplification") — **Advancer; Dirimens Copulatio; Incrementum; Progressio.** Words or clauses placed in climactic order; opposite of **Meiosis:**
 "I may, I must, I can, I will, I doe
 Leave following that which it is gaine to misse."
             (Sidney, *Astrophil and Stella*, XLVII)

Avancer. Puttenham's term for **Auxesis.**

Aversio (a VER si o; L. "turning away") — **Apostrophe.**

Barbaralexis (bar bar a LEX is) — **Barbarismus.**

Barbarismus (bar bar IS mus; G. "foreign mode of speech") —

Barbaralexis; Forrein Speech.
1. Unnatural words or mispronunciation:
> SIR HUGH EVANS: Fery goot: I will make a prief of it
> in my note-book; and we will after-
> words ork upon the cause with as
> great discreetly as we can."
> *(Merry Wives of Windsor,* I, i)

2. Wrenched accent to fit meter or rhyme:
> "But — Oh! ye lords of ladies intellectual,
> Inform us truly, have they not hen-peck'd you all?"
> (Byron, *Don Juan,* I, xxii)

Bathos (BA thos; G. "depth"). *See* **Pathos.**

Bdelygma (bdel YG ma; G. "nausea, sickness; filth, nastiness") —
Abominatio. Expression of hatred, usually short. As Emilia to
Othello:
> "O gull! O dolt!
> As ignorant as dirt."
> *(Othello,* V, ii)

Benedictio (ben e DIC ti o; L. "extolling, praising, lauding") —
Eulogia.

Benevolentia (ben e VO LEN ti a) — **Philophronesis.**

Bitter Taunt. Puttenham's term for **Sarcasmus.**

Blazon — **Effictio.**

Bomphiologia (bom phi o LO gi a; G. "booming, buzzing words");
alt. sp. **Bomphilogia** — **Pompous Speech.** Bombastic speech:
> " 'Solus,' egregious dog? O viper vile!
> The 'solus' in thy most mervailous face;
> The 'solus' in thy teeth, and in thy throat,
> And in thy hateful lungs, yea, in thy maw, perdy,
> And, which is worse, within thy nasty mouth!
> I do retort the 'solus' in thy bowels;
> For I can take, and Pistol's cock is up,
> And flashing fire will follow."
> *(Henry V,* II, i)

See also **Periergia.**

Brachylogia (bra chy LO gi a; G. "brevity in speech or writing") — **Asyndeton; Cutted Comma.** *See also* **Praegnans Constructio.**
1. Omission of conjunctions between words: "Beguil'd, di-
vorced, wronged, spited, slain!"

2. Brevity of diction; abbreviated construction; word or words omitted. A modern theorist differentiated this use from **Ellipsis,** *q.v.*, in that the elements missing are more subtly, less artificially, omitted in ellipsis: "The corps goeth before, we follow after, we come to the grave, she is put into the fire, a lamentation is made" (Peacham).

Brevitas (BRE vi tas; L. "shortness"). Concise expression.

Broad Floute. Puttenham's term for **Antiphrasis.**

Cacemphaton (cac EM pha ton; G. "ill-sounding, equivocal") — **Aischrologia; Turpis Locutio; Foule Speech.**

1. Scurrilous jest; lewd allusion or "double entendre": "as one that would say to a young woman, *I pray you let me jape with you,* which indeed is no more but let me sport with you" (Puttenham).
2. Sounds combined for harsh effect. So Peacham: "when there come many syllables of one sound together in one sentence, like a continual jarring upon one string, thus, neither honour nor nobility, could move a naughty niggardly noddy."

Cacosistaton (cac o SIS ta ton; G. "badly constructed"). An argument that can serve as well on either side of a question.

Cacosyntheton (cac o SYN the ton; G. "incorrect connection of words") — **Male Collocatum; Misplacer.**

1. Awkward transposition of the parts of a sentence.
2. The misunderstanding that often occurs from (1):"A foolish fellow when I saw before the king, stand laughing."

(Peacham)

See also **Hysteron Proteron.**

Cacozelia (cac o ZE li a; G. "unhappy imitation") — **Fonde Affectation.** Studied affectation of style; affected diction made up of adaptation of Latin words or inkhorn terms, as when Hamlet parodies Osric:

"Sir, his definement suffers no perdition in you; though, I know, to divide him inventorially would dozy th' arithmetic of memory, and yet but yaw neither in respect of his quick sail. But, in the verity of extolment, I take him to be a soul of great article, and his infusion of such dearth and rareness as, to make true diction of him, his semblable is his mirror, and who else would trace him, his umbrage, nothing more. . . . The concernancy, sir? Why do we wrap the gentleman in our rawer breath?"

(Hamlet, V, ii)

See also **Soriasmus.**

Caesum (CAE sum; L. "something cut off") — **Comma.**

Canonical Syllogism. The irreducible common form of the various types of syllogism, either universal or particular.

Caresyntheton — Hyperbaton.

Casu Pro Casu (CA su; L. "one case for another") — **Antiptosis.**

Catachresis (cat a CHRE sis; G. "misuse, misapplication") — **Abusio; Abuse.**

1. Implied metaphor, using words wrenched from common usage, as when Hamlet says, "I will speak daggers to her."
2. A second definition which seems slightly different but perhaps is not: an extravagant, unexpected, farfetched metaphor, as when a weeping woman's eyes become Niagara Falls.

Catacosmesis (cat a cos ME sis; G. "downward arrangement, order"). Opposite of **Climax;** ordering words from greatest to least in dignity. Some see an unwitting instance in the Yale motto: "For God, for Country, and for Yale."

Cataplexis (cat a PLEX is; G. "amazement"). A threatening of punishment, misfortune, or disaster:

> "Hence
> Horrible villain! or I'll spurn thine eyes
> Like balls from me; I'll unhair thy head!
> Thou shall be whipp'd with wire, and stow'd in brine,
> Smarting in ling'ring pickle."

(Antony and Cleopatra, II, v)

See also **Paraenesis; Ominatio.**

Categoria (cat e go RI a; G. "accusation, assertion, prediction")— **Accusatio.** Reproaching a person with his wickedness to his face:

> "Now when even was come, he was setting at meat with the twelve disciples; and as they were eating, he said, Verily, I say unto you, that one of you shall betray me."

(Matt. 26:20–21)

Categorical Propositions.

Four forms:

> Universal Affirmative: All policemen are stupid.
> Universal Negative: No policeman is stupid.

Particular Affirmative: Some policemen are stupid.

Particular Negative: Some policemen are not stupid.

Quality of proposition: Affirmative or Negative.

Quantity of proposition: Universal or Particular.

Also called "Simple" propositions, as opposed to Disjunctive and Hypothetical, which are called "Compound."

Categorical Syllogism. One that contains **Categorical Propositions,** *q.v.* exclusively. It can contain only three terms:

Major Premise.

Minor Premise.

Conclusion.

Causes. Logicians distinguish four:

1. Material (for example, the metal from which a car is made).
2. Formal (the design of the car).
3. Efficient (the assembling of the car).
4. Final (the purpose of the car: transportation).

Ceratin (cer A tin). An argument so couched that, seemingly, all possibilities equally prove it true (or false). A variety of **Dilemma,** *q.v.*

Ceratinae (cer A tin ae; G. "made of horn"). The "horns" of a **Dilemma,** *q.v.*

Certitudo (cer ti TU do; L. "certainty") — **Asphalia.**

Changeling. Puttenham's term for **Hypallage.**

Characterismus (cha rac ter IS mus; G. "marking with a distinctive sign"). Type of **Energia,** *q.v.*; description of the body or mind. *See* **Effictio,** for example.

Charientismus (cha ri en TIS mus; G. "wit, graceful jest") — **Privie Nippe.** Type of **Irony;** clothing a disagreeable sense with agreeable expressions; soothing over a difficulty, or turning aside antagonism with a joke:

"KING: Have you heard the argument? Is there no of-
      fense in't?

HAMLET: No, no, they do but jest, poison in jest;
      no offence i' the world."

                              (*Hamlet,* III, ii)

Chiasmus (chi AS mus; G. "crossing") — **Antimetabole; Commutatio.** The term is derived from the Greek letter X (chi) whose shape, if the two halves of the construction are rendered in separate verses, it resembles:

"Polish'd in courts, and harden'd in the field
Renown'd for conquest, and in council skill'd."
(Addison, "The Campaign")

Chleuasmos (chleu AS mos; G ."mockery, irony") — **Epicertomesis.** A sarcastic reply that mocks an opponent and leaves him
no answer.

> "DON JUAN (placidly): . . . Yes: a funeral was al-
> ways a festivity in black, especially the funeral of a
> relative. At all events, family ties are rarely kept up
> here. Your father is quite accustomed to this: he will
> not expect any devotion from you.
> ANA. Wretch: I wore mourning for him all my life.
> DON JUAN: Yes: it became you."
> (Bernard Shaw, *Man and Superman*, III)

Chorographia (chor o GRAPH i a). Description of a nation. *See
also* **Prosopographia; Topographia; Chronographia; Geographia;
Hydrographia; Anemographia; Dendrographia.**

> "This royal throne of kings, this scepter'd isle,
> This earth of majesty, this seat of Mars,
> This other Eden, demi-paradise,
> This fortress built by Nature for herself
> Against infection and the hand of war,
> This happy breed of men, this little world,
> This precious stone set in the silver sea,
> Which serves it in the office of a wall
> Or as a moat defensive to a house,
> Against the envy of less happier lands,
> This blessed plot, this earth, this realm, this England. . . ."
> (*Richard II*, II, i)

Chria (CHRI a; G. rhet. "pregnant sentence or maxim, often il-
lustrated by an anecdote").

1. A short exposition of a deed or saying of a person whose
   name is mentioned: "Scipio was wont to say, he was never
   less idle, than when he was void of the commonwealth mat-

ters, and never less alone than when he was alone" (Sherry).

2. A short rhetorical exercise in which a maxim or moral observation is developed and varied, often through the traditional seven parts of an oration.

Chronographia (chro no GRAPH i a; G. "time-writing"). Type of **Energia,** *q.v.*; **Counterfait Time.** Description of time as when Romeo says:

> "Look love, what envious streaks
> Do lace the severing clouds in yonder East.
> Night's candles are burnt out, and jocund day
> Stands tiptoe on the misty mountain tops."
>
> (*Romeo and Juliet,* III, v)

See also **Prosopographia; Topographia; Chorographia; Geographia; Hydrographia; Anemographia; Dendrographia.**

Ciceronian Style. The phrase has been used in many ways. It has meant the oratorical style, par excellence; the style that makes maximum use of the period; the full, or amplified, style; the "pure" style of Cicero's orations, which English Humanists aimed to imitate — the touchstone, that is, of classical Latinity; the ornamental, or Asiatic, style, one that uses the "schemes of thought" (*see* **Trope**). Cf. **Senecan Style; Period.**

Circuitio (cir cu IT i o; L. "going around") — **Periphrasis.**

Circumductum (cir cum DUC tum). Latin equivalent of **Colon.**

Circumitio (cir cum IT i o) — **Periphrasis.**

Circumlocution (L. "to speak around") — **Periphrasis.**

Civill Jest. Puttenham's term for **Asteismus.**

Clausula (CLAU su la).

1. The conclusion or cadence of a **Period.**
2. A logically concluded utterance; what we would call a sentence.

Climax (G. "ladder") — **Gradatio; Ascendus; Methalemsis; Marching Figure.** Mounting by degrees through words or sentences of increasing weight and in parallel construction: "Labour getteth learning, learning getteth fame, fame getteth honour, honour getteth bliss forever" (Wilson).

See also **Auxesis; Anadiplosis.**

Close Conceit. Puttenham's term for **Noema.**

Coacervatio (co ac er VAT i o; L. "heaping together"). Opposite of **Epitrochasmus.**

Cohortatio (co hor TA ti o; L. "exhortation"). Amplification that moves the hearer's indignation, as when the horrors of an enemy's barbarities are dwelt upon to promote patriotism.

Colon (G. "limb; clause") — **Circumductum; Member; Membrum Orationis.** The second of the three elements in the classical theory of the Period, an (originally Peripatetic) theory of prose rhythm. More generally an independent clause that yet depends on the remainder of the sentence for its meaning. Halfway between a **Comma** and a **Period,** *q.g.v.*

Colors [*of rhetoric*].

1. Sometimes, generally, all the figures.
2. More narrowly, and usually, the **Easy Ornaments** or the schemes. Perhaps the colors might be most appropriately defined as a general term for devices used as superficial decoration (rather than metaphorical creation of meaning) of a discourse. *See* **Difficult Ornaments.**
3. Quintilian uses the Latin word "color" to mean the particular slant or gloss one seeks to give an argument or a sequence of events.

Comma (G. "that which is cut off, e.g., short clause") — **Caesum; Dependens; Incisum; Hypodiastole.** The first and shortest of the three elements in the classical theory of the period, an (originally Peripatetic) theory of prose rhythm. More generally, in Greek and Latin prose theory, a short phrase or dependent clause. Cf. **Colon** and **Period.**

Commemoratio (com mem or A ti o; L. "to bring to remembrance") — **Apomnemonysis.**

Commendatio (com men DA ti o) — **Encomium.**

Commentatio (com men TA ti o; L. "study; careful preparation") — **Enthymeme.**

Commentum (com MEN tum) — **Enthymeme.**

Commonplaces. See 2.3.7.

Commoratio (com mor A ti o; L. "dwelling, tarrying") — **Abode.** Emphasizing a strong point by repeating it several times in different words: ". . . expelled, thrust out, banished, and cast away from the city" (Peacham).

Communio (com MUN i o) — **Synonymia.**

Commutatio (com mu TA ti o; L. "change, interchange") — **Chiasmus,** *q.v.*; **Antimetabole.** Order of the first clause is reversed in the second: "We must not live to eat, but eat to live."

Compar (COM par; L. "like, equal") — **Isocolon.**

Comparison — **Comparatio.** Showing similarities between persons or things, like or seemingly unlike. It can be figure or argument. *See also* **Syncrisis.**

> "The simple inherit folly: but the prudent are crowned
> with knowledge."
>
> (Proverbs 14:18)

Compensatio (com pen SAT i o; L. "weighing, balancing").
1. **Antisagoge.**
2. **Antanagoge.**

Complexio (com PLEX i o; L. "combination, connection").
1. **Symploce.**
2. **Synaloepha.**

Compliment. Performance of affected ceremonies in words, looks, or gestures.

Composition (L. "putting together"). In rhetoric it is sometimes used as a general term for word arrangement. The Greek equivalent term is **Synthesis,** the Latin **Compositio.**

Compound Proposition. One that contains two elements.

Comprehension (L. "seizing with the hands") — **Symploce.**

Comprobatio (com pro BA ti o; L. "approval"). Complimenting one's judges or hearers to win their confidence.

> "I therefore say to thee, (O Just Judge) that I and only
> I was the worker of *Basilius* death. They were these
> hands that gave him that poisonous potion that brought
> death unto him and Loss to *Arcadia*."
>
> (Sidney, *Old Arcadia*, V)

Concessio (con CESS i o; L. "allowing, granting") — **Permissio; Epitrope.** The speaker concedes a point either to hurt the adversary directly or to prepare for a more important argument:

> "FALSTAFF: Boy, tell him I am deaf.
>
> PAGE: You must speak louder. My master is deaf.
>
> JUSTICE: I am sure he is, to the hearing of anything
>   good."
>
> (*II Henry IV*, I, ii)

See also **Synchoresis.**

Conciliatio (con cil i A ti o) — **Synoeciosis; Euphemismus** (2).

Conclusio (con CLU si o; L. "shutting up, closing").
1. **Period.**
2. A brief summary.

See **Peroration.**

Conductio (con DUC ti o; L. "bringing together") — **Synathroesmus.**

Conduplicatio (con du pli CAT i o; L. "doubling, repetition"). Repetition of a word or words in succeeding clauses (1) for amplification or (2) to express emotion:
1. "You are promoting riots, Gracchus, yes, civil and internal riots."
2. "You were not moved when his mother embraced your knees? You were not moved?"
                    (*Rhetorica ad Herennium,* IV, 38)

Conexio (co NEX i o; L. "binding together, close union") — **Ploce.**

Conexum (co NEX um) — **Symploce.**

Confirmation — Amplificatio. The fifth part of the seven-part classical oration. This was the main part of the speech, the one in which the pros and cons of the argument were brought out.

Conformatio (con for MA ti o; L. "symmetrical forming") — **Prosopopoeia.**

Confutation — Refutation.

Congeries (CON ge ries; L. "heap, pile") — **Synathroesmus.**

Conglobatio (con glo BA ti o; L. "gathering into a globe or ball") — **Systrophe.**

Conjunctio (con JUNC ti o; L. "joining together"). Clauses or phrases expressing similar ideas are held together by placing the verb between them: "Either with disease physical beauty fades, or with age" (*Rhetorica ad Herennium,* IV, xxvii, 38).

Consenting Close. Puttenham's term for **Epiphonema.**

Consolatio (con so LA ti o; L. "consoling, comforting") — **Paramythia.**

Consonance. Resemblance of stressed consonant-sounds where the associated vowels differ: "Roger Ringler raised a ruckus." The term has also been taken to mean a kind of reverse alliteration, in which terminal rather than initial consonants are repeated. An example might be: "Bill shall call the girl."
See also **Alliteration.**

Constantia (con STANT i a; L. "steadiness, firmness") — **Eustathia.**

Constitutio (con sti TU ti o) — **Issue.**

Consummatio (con sum MA ti o; L. "casting up, summing up") — **Diallage.**

Contentio (con TEN ti o).
1. **Antithesis.**
2. **Antistasis.**

Continuatio (con tin u A ti o; L. "connection, continuation").
1. **Period.**
2. "A continual heaping of words" (Sherry); a long, full sentence:

> "And if fortune may do much against them, which
> hath put all their accounts upon chance: all are
> not to be committed to fortune, lest fortune have
> too great a domination upon them."

> (Sherry)

Contractio (con TRAC ti o; L. "bringing together") — **Systole.**

Contradictories. Two mutually exclusive propositions: they cannot *both* be true; they cannot *both* be false:

> All judges are lawyers.
> Some judges are not lawyers.

Contraposition — Antithesis.

Contraries. Two propositions that cannot both be true, though they may both be false:

> All policemen are stupid.
> No policeman is stupid.

Contrarium (con TRAR i um) — **Enantiosis** (2). One of two opposite statements is used to prove the other: "Now how should you expect one who has ever been hostile to his own interests to be friendly to another's?" (*Rhetorica ad Herennium*, IV, xviii, 25).

Conversio (con VER si o; L. "turning around") — **Antistrophe** (1).

Conversum (con VER sum) — **Conversio.**

Coople Clause. Puttenham's term for **Polysyndeton.**

Copulatio (cop u LA ti o; L. "coupling, joining") — **Ploce.**

Correctio (cor REC ti o; L. "making straight, setting right").
1. **Epanorthosis; Epidiorthosis; Epitimesis; Diorismos.** *See also* **Metanoia.** Correction of a word or phrase used previously: "I perish of love, no not so much perish as live in mortal pain."
2. **Diorthosis; Prodiorthosis; Praecedens Correctio.** Preparing the way for saying something the speaker knows will be unpleasant to his auditors: "Although I realize how offensive this will sound, it is something that must be said."

Counterchange. Puttenham's term for **Antimetabole.**

Counterfait Action. Puttenham's term for **Pragmatographia.**

Counterfait Countenance. Puttenham's term for **Prosopographia.**

Counterfait in Personation. Puttenham's term for **Prosopopoeia.**
Counterfait Place. Puttenham's term for **Topographia.**
Counterfait Representation. Puttenham's term for **Hypotyposis.**
Counterfait Time. Puttenham's term for **Chronographia.**
Counterturne. Puttenham's term for **Antistrophe** (1).
Crocodillinae (croc o DIL li nae) — **Crocodilities.** A kind of **Dilemma,** *q.v.*:

> "A crocodile, having seized a woman's son, said that
> he would restore him, if she would tell him the truth.
> She replied, 'you will not restore him.' Was it the croc-
> odile's duty to give him up?"
> (Quintilian, I, x, 5 n.2)

Crosse-Couple. Puttenham's term for **Synoeciosis.**
Cuckowspell. Puttenham's term for **Epizeuxis.**
Cumulatio (cum u LAT i o; L. "forming into a heap") — **Sorias-mus.**
Curry Favell. Puttenham's term for **Euphemism** (2). A "curry-favell" once meant "a flatterer," whence our corrupted version, "curry favor."
Cursus (CUR sus). The "system of rhythmical clause endings employed in the composition of the Latin prayers of the Church during the best periods of liturgical art" (Croll, *Style, Rhetoric, and Rhythm*, p. 303). There were three basic patterns or runs: *cursus planus, cursus tardus,* and *cursus velox.* "According to medieval theory, the *cursus* was used at the ends of the *commata, cola,* and *periodus* (or *conclusio*), the parts, large or small, of which a rhetorical period is constructed. In other words it was a conventional way of giving a beautiful flow at the end of a rhetorical unit" (Croll, *Style, Rhetoric, and Rhythm*, p. 306). The *planus*, or even run, consisted of a dactyl and a trochee; the *tardus*, or slow run, of two dactyls; the *velox*, or quick run, of a dactyl and two trochees.
Curt Style — **Senecan Style.**
Cutted Comma. Puttenham's term for **Brachylogia.**
Declamatio (de cla MA ti o). The elaborately ornamental and rehearsed speech, usually on a fictional law case, which formed a central part of Roman rhetorical discipline.
Declinatio (de clin A ti o; L. "bending aside"). A digression.
Decorum (L. "propriety") — **To Prepon.** Fittingness in matters of language and usage; under it one might subsume all Aristotle's

pleas to suit style to subject and to audience, arguments to audience, gestures and voice to style, etc.

Deesis (de E sis; f. L. "god") — **Obtestatio.** Vehement supplication either to the gods or to men. *See also* **Ecphonesis; Donysis.**

> "O ye heavens, which continually keep the Course allotted unto you, can none of your Influences prevail so much upon the miserable *Ginecia,* as to make her preserve a Course so long embraced by her?"
>
> (Sidney, *Old Arcadia,* II)

Default. Puttenham's term for **Ellipsis.**

Definer by Difference. Puttenham's term for **Horismus.**

Definiendum (de fin i EN dum). The term to be defined in a definition.

Definiens (de FIN i ens). The defining terms or categories in a definition; they are usually called the genus term and the species term. Thus man (**Definiendum**) is defined by calling him "a rational (species) animal (genus)."

Definitio (de fi NI ti o; L. "boundary, limitation") — **Horismus; Exposition.**

Definition.

Two Parts:

definiens — defining term.

definiendum — term to be defined.

Some common traditional types:

prescriptive — insistence that a certain definition is the only one acceptable.

stipulative — an agreement that one of several meanings will be intended for purposes of a single debate or discourse.

lexical — as in a dictionary.

negative — defining something by proving what it is not.

likeness/difference.

classificatory — assigning the object to the smallest possible class. A classifying definition based on internal qualities is sometimes called "essential"; one based on externals, "descriptive." It is difficult, sometimes, to distinguish between them.

An adequate definition of "definition," one that would satisfactorily compensate for the deficiencies of the traditional ones, is beyond the scope of this list and of its compiler. As a partial expansion of the traditional categories just given, though, perhaps the by now old warning of Ogden and Richards (*The Meaning of Meaning,* pp. 109 ff.) may be suggestive.

"There is at present no theory of Definition capable of practical application under normal circumstances. The traditional theory, insofar as it has not been lost in the barren subtleties of Genus and Differentia, and in the confusion due to the term 'Connotation,' has made little progress — chiefly on account of the barbarous superstitions about language which have gathered on the confines of logic from the earliest times. Four difficulties have stood in the way and must first be removed."

The first of these difficulties is this: do we define words or things? The answer suggested would seem to be that we define words by suggesting synonyms, things by enumerating their properties and contrasting those properties with the properties of other things. The second of the difficulties is really a caution not to confuse the two kinds of definition distinguished in the first. The third insists that "all definitions are essentially *ad hoc*." "They are," these authors explain, "relevant to some purpose or situation, and consequently are applicable only over a restricted field or 'universe of discourse.' " Taken out of the field of discourse for which it was intended, the definition becomes a metaphor ("energy" for the physicist, and "energy" or the lack of it, as the schoolmaster sees it in his pupils, is the example used). The fourth difficulty is the "problem of 'intensive' as opposed to 'extensive' definition which comes to a head with the use of the terms 'denote' and 'connote.' "

". . . two symbols may be said to have the same connotation when they symbolize the same reference. An intensive or connotative definition will be one which involves no change in those characters of a referent in virtue of which it forms a context with its original sign. In an extensive definition there may be such a change. In other words when we define intensively we keep to the same sign-situation for definiendum and definiens; when we define extensively this may be changed."

Dehortatio (de hor TA ti o). Dissuasion; advice to the contrary:
> "Confess yourself to heaven;
> Repent what's past; avoid what is to come;
> And do not spread the compost on the weeds,
> To make them ranker."
>   (*Hamlet*, III, iv)

Deliberatio (de lib er A ti o). Evaluating possible courses of action; weighing arguments:

> ". . . whom shall I blame? what shall I pretend? shall I make learning hateful to you by my reprehensions, shall I make my silence accessory to your idleness? It is not in my power, it is in your discretion to reform it."
>
> (Hoskyns)

Delivery. That part of rhetorical theory which teaches control of voice, effective gesture, pose.

Demonstratio (de mon STRA ti o; L. "pointing out, showing") — **Vision.** Vivid description.

Dendrographia. Description of trees. *See also* **Prosopographia; Topographia; Chorographia; Chronographia; Geographia; Hydrographia; Anemographia.** So Joyce Kilmer:

> "I think that I shall never see
> A poem as lovely as a tree.
> A tree whose hungry mouth is prest
> Against the sweet earth's flowing breast." etc.

Denominatio (de nom i NA ti o) — **Metonymy.**

Denumeratio (de num e RA ti o; L. "enumeration"). Amplifying a general fact or idea by giving all of its details. *See also* **Congeries; Diaeresis; Digestion; Distribution; Enumeration.** Sidney both gives all of the details — and talks about giving all of the details — of his woe in *Astrophil and Stella*, LVIII:

> "Doubt there hath bene, when with his golden chaine
> The Oratour so farre men's harts doth bind,
> That no pace else their guided steps can find,
> But as he them more short or slacke doth raine,
> Whether with words this soveraignty he gaine,
> Cloth'd with fine tropes, with strongest reasons lin'd,
> Or else pronouncing grace, wherewith his mind
> Prints his owne lively forme in rudest braine.
> Now judge by this: in piercing phrases late,
> Th'anatomy of all my woes I wrate,
> *Stella's* sweet breath the same to me did reed.
> O voice, o face, maugre my speeche's might,
> Which wooed wo, most ravishing delight
> Even those sad words even in sad me did breed."

Denying the Antecedent (Fallacy of). To deny the antecedent, or first part, of a hypothetical proposition:

If John ran a four-minute mile he is a fast miler.
John did not run a four-minute mile.
Therefore, John is not a fast miler.

Dependens (de PEN dens; L. "hanging from") — **Comma.**

Descriptio (de SCRIP ti o) — **Energia.**

Diabole (di A bo le; G. "false accusation, slander," from "to throw across"). A prediction of (and sometimes a denunciation of) things that are to take place in the future:

"Then he took unto him the twelve, and said unto them, Behold, we go up to Jerusalem, and all things that are written by the prophets concerning the Son of man shall be accomplished. For he shall be delivered unto the Gentiles, and shall be mocked, and spitefully entreated, and spitted on: And they shall scourge him, and put him to death: and the third day he shall rise again."

(Luke 18:31–33)

Diacope (di A co pe; G. "cleft, gash").

1. **Tmesis.** Repetition of a word with one or a few words in between: "My heart is fixed, O God, my heart is fixed" (Peacham).
2. **Dieremenon; Disparsum.** Separation of the elements of a compound word by another word or words: "West — by God — Virginia."

Diaeresis (di AER e sis; G. "dividing, division") — **Partitio.**

1. Dividing the genus into species in order to amplify.
    "The king-becoming graces,
    As justice, verity, temp'rance, stableness,
    Bounty, perseverance, mercy, lowliness,
    Devotion, patience, courage, fortitude."
                    (*Macbeth*, IV, iii)
2. Dividing one syllable into two, especially by pronouncing two adjacent vowels, as in preëminent; also the twin dots used above a letter to indicate such a pronunciation.
3. In prosody: the division made in a line or a verse when the end of a foot coincides with the end of a word.

Dialectic. *See* **Rhetoric.**

Dialelumenon (di a le LU men on).

1. **Asyndeton.**
2. Conversational style.

Diallage (di AL la ge; G. "interchange") — **Consummatio.**
Bringing several arguments to establish a single point.

Dialogismus (di a log IS mus; G. "debate, discussion") — **Right Reasoner.** Speaking in another man's person. *See also* **Prosopopoeia.**

> ". . . if we should fain king Edward the third, understanding how his successor Queen Mary had lost the town of Calais by negligence, should say: That which the sword won, the distaff hath lost."
>
> (Puttenham)

Dialysis (di AL y sis; G. "separation, dissolution").

1. **Dismembrer.** A figure in which one argues from a series of disjunctive (compound hypothetical) propositions (e.g.: "Either Bill ran out of gas or he ran out of money") directly to a conclusion. Henry V says before Agincourt:

> "If we are mark'd to die, we are enow
> To do our country loss; and if to live,
> The fewer men, the greater share the honour.
> God's will! I pray thee wish not one man more."

See also **Dilemma** (2).

2. *See* **Divisio.** A statement of a problem followed by particularization of the alternatives; type of divisio:

> "Answer him fair with yea, or nay,
> If it be yea: I shall be fain.
> If it be nay: friends as before."
>
> (Wyatt)

Dialyton (di A ly ton; G. "dissolved").

1. **Asyndeton.**
2. May also mean — generally — emphasizing a word by setting it off from the rest of the sentence in other ways besides asyndeton.

Diaphora (di APH or a; G. "dislocation, difference, disagreement").

1. **Ploce.**
2. Peacham: Repetition of a common word rather than a proper name to signify qualities of the person as well as naming him; as when Desdemona says:

> "My advocation is not now in tune.
> My lord is not my lord."
>
> (*Othello*, III, iv)

Diaporesis (di a por E sis; G. "being at a loss, doubting") — **Aporia.**

Diastole (di AST o le; G. "drawing asunder, separation") —
Eciasis. Lengthening a syllable or vowel usually short.
Diasyrmus (di a SYR mus; G. "disparagement, ridicule") —
Elevatio. Disparagement of opponent's argument through a base
similitude. *See also* **Apodioxis.** "He fights with leaden daggers;
i.e., he has weak arguments" (Peacham).
Diatyposis (di a typ o sis; G. "vivid description").
 1. **Energia.**
 2. **Testamentum.** Recommending useful precepts to someone
    else (Peacham's definition), as in Polonius' advice to
    Laertes (*Hamlet*, I, iii).
Diazeugma (di a ZEUG ma; G. "disjoining"). One subject with
many verbs:
>   "he bites his lip and starts;
>   Stops on a sudden, looks upon the ground,
>   Then lays his finger on his temple; straight
>   Springs out into fast gait, then stops again. . . ."
>   (*Henry VIII*, III, ii)
Dicacologia (di cae o LO gi a; G. "plea in defence"); alt. sp.
Dichologia — Anangeon; Excuse. Defending one's words or acts
with reasonable excuses; excusing by necessity; defending the
justice of one's cause as briefly as possible:
>   "I forsook my friend, but the laws compelled me. I
>   kept friendship most faithfully as long as the laws
>   permitted me, and now I am not cast off by will, but
>   by force of law."
>   (Peacham)
Dictamen (dic TA men) — **Ars Dictaminis.**
Dicremenon (di e RE men on) — **Diacope** (2).
Difficult Ornaments — Ornatus Difficilis. The distinction between easy and difficult ornaments parallels that often made between **Schemes** and **Tropes**: the easy ornaments were those that
involved superficial patterns of sound or arrangement; the hard
ornaments involved some real change in meaning, some metaphorical substitution. As with scheme and trope, it is easy to
distinguish extremes. **Alliteration** is easy, **Synecdoche** difficult or hard. But distinction is harder with various kinds of
Paronomasia, for example. It may be generally acceptable to say
that the easy ornaments were ornaments pure and simple; the
difficult ones effected a fundamental change in meaning. *Rhetorica ad Herennium* lists ten difficult figures: **Onomatopoeia,**

Antonomasia, Metonymy, Periphrasis, Hyperbaton, Hyperbole, Synecdoche, Catachresis, Metaphor, Allegory. Examples of easy ornaments would be various devices of repetition of both letter and word. (See chap. 4.)

Digestion. *See* **Enumeration.** An orderly enumeration of the points to be discussed, the implications of a question, etc.

Digression — Parecbasis; Egressio; Excessus; Excursus; Stragler. The various terms have both a technical and a general meaning. The technical: the tale, or interpolated anecdote, which follows the exposition and illustrates or amplifies some point in it. Quintilian thinks the position of the anecdote after the exposition is not crucial. The general: any digressive tale or interpolation, especially one prepared in advance on a commonplace subject, and inserted at the appropriate time.

Dilemma (G. "double proposition"). *See also* **Ceratin.**

1. General Definition: Any technique of argument which offers an opponent a choice, or a series of them, all of which are unacceptable. The counterargument ("taking the dilemma by the horns") is to deny the premise by which choice is restricted to unacceptable alternatives. For example, the boss argues: I will not give you a raise; either it will make you lazy and less efficient, or avaricious and less content. The employee replies: No, it will make me more energetic, because less discontent.

2. Logic. *See* **Dialysis.** *See also* **Compound Proposition; Hypothetical Proposition; Disjunctive Proposition; Categorical Proposition.** A syllogism in which the major premise is a compound hypothetical proposition and the minor a disjunctive proposition. If the conclusion is a disjunctive proposition, the syllogism is called *complex*; if the conclusion is a categorical proposition, *simple*. For example, if the welfare legislation feeds the people, they will grow lazy; if it does not feed the people, it will be a failure. It either will or will not feed the people. Therefore, the legislation will either make people lazy or it will be a failure. A dilemma with the minor premise left out makes the figure **Dialysis,** *q.v.*

Diminutio (di min U ti o; L. "lessening") — **Litotes.**

Dinumeratio (di nu mer A ti o; L. "reckoning up") — **Diaeresis.**

Diorismos (di or IS mos; G. "distinction, definition") — **Correctio** (1).

Diorthosis (di or THO sis; G. "making straight") — **Correctio** (2).
Director. Puttenham's term for **Gnome.**
Dirimens Copulatio (DIR i mens cop u LA ti o; L. "breaking off or interrupting a conversation").
   1. Adding a point to balance what has already been said:
     "For he is the minister of God to thee for good.
     But if thou do that which is evil, be afraid; for
     he beareth not the sword in vain: for he is the
     minister of God, a revenger to execute wrath
     upon him that doeth evil. Wherefore ye must needs
     be subject, not only for wrath, but also for con-
     science sake."
                   (Romans 13:4–5)
   2. **Auxesis.** Building toward a climax.
Disabler. Puttenham's term for **Meiosis.**
Disdainefull. Puttenham's term for **Insultatio.**
Disjunctio (dis JUNC ti o; L. "separation").
   1. Use of different verbs to express similar ideas in successive clauses, as when one says: "He who excuses himself, accuses himself" (Gabriel Meronier, *Tresor des Sentences*).
   2. Logic: the relation between two or more alternatives of a disjunctive proposition.
   3. The conclusion of each proposition with its own verb, as in "better to give than to receive, to sow than to reap." Opposite of **Adjunctio**, *q.v.*
Disjunctive Proposition (Disjunction). A proposition composed of two propositions, one of which must be true and the other of which sometimes may be true: "Either Bill ran out of money, or his car broke down."
Disjunctive (or Alternative) Syllogism. One containing a disjunctive proposition: "Either his car broke down or he forgot our appointment."
Dismembrer. Puttenham's term for **Dialysis.**
Disparsum (dis PAR sum; L. "scattered, dispersed") — **Diacope** (2).
Dispositio (dis po SI ti o) — **Arrangement.**
Dissimilitude (L. "unlikeness") — **Syncrisis.**
Dissimulatio (dis sim u LA ti o; L. "disguise, concealment") — **Irony.**
Dissolutio (dis so LU ti o) — **Asyndeton.**

Distinctio (dis TINC ti o) — **Paradiastole.** Explicit reference to various meanings of a word, thereby removing ambiguities: "Remove all scruples with distinction, as being charged that you have brought very light reasons, you may answer if by *light* you mean *clear*, I am glad you do see them; if by light you mean *of no weight*, I am sorry you do not feel them" (Hoskyns).

Distributed Term (of a Syllogism). Refers to all members of a class designated by a term.

Distribution — Merismus; Distributor. Dividing the whole into its parts; type of **Divisio,** *q.v.*

> "Two things he feared, but the third was death;
> That fierce youngmans vnruly maistery;
> His money, which he lou'd as liuing breath;
> And his faire wife, whom honest long he kept vneath."
>
> (Spenser, *Faerie Queene,* III, x, 2)

Divisio (di VI si o). Division into kinds or classes. *See also* **Distribution; Dialysis.**

> "Is it her nature or is it her will,
>   to be so cruell to an humbled foe?
>   if nature, then she may it mcnd with skill,
>   if will, then she at will may will forgoe."
>
> (Spenser, *Amoretti,* XLI)

Domain (of a Proposition). The group of all entities that can serve as the subject of a proposition. Thus in the proposition: ——— loves Joan, all those who might love Joan are the domain of the proposition. Entities that would render the proposition nonsensical or false are usually excluded from the domain (e.g., "apples" in the proposition above). More largely, we might say that the domain of the argument is that class of objects about which the argument can make a meaningful statement.

Donysis (DON y sis; G. "to disturb, agitate"). Describing or re-enacting strong emotions: fear, anger, madness, etc. *See also* **Ecphonesis; Deesis.**

Doubler. Puttenham's term for **Ploce.**

Double Supply. Puttenham's term for **Syllepsis.**

Doublet — Epizeuxis.

Doubtfull. Puttenham's term for **Aporia.**

Drie Mock. Puttenham's term for **Irony.**

Dubitatio (du bi TA ti o; L. "wavering in opinion") — **Aporia.**

Duplicatio (du pli CA ti o) — **Anadiplosis.**

Easy Ornaments — Ornatus Facilis. Opposite of **Difficult Ornaments,** *q.v.* See also chapter 4.

Eccho Sounde. Puttenham's term for **Epanalepsis.**

Eciasis (ec I a sis) — **Diastole.**

Eclipsis (e CLIP sis; G. "to leave out"); alt. sp. of **Ellipsis,** *q.v.*

Ecphonesis (ec pho NE sis; G. "to cry out"); alt. sp. **Ecphonema — Exclamatio; Epiphonesis; Outcrie.** Exclamation expressing emotion. (Presumably would most often be equivalent to **Apostrophe.**)

Ecphrasis (EC phra sis; G. "description").

1. A self-contained description, often on a commonplace subject, which can be inserted at a fitting place in a discourse (derived from 2).
2. **Energia.**

Effictio (ef FIC ti o; L. "fashioning") — **Blazon.** Personal description (outward appearance); the head-to-toe itemization of a heroine's charms, common in earlier English poetry:

"My Lady's hair is threads of beaten gold,
Her front the purest Chrystal eye hath seen:
Her eyes the brightest stars the heavens hold,
Her cheeks red roses such as seld have been:
Her pretty lips of red vermillion dye,
Her hands of ivory the purest white:
Her blush Aurora, or the morning sky,
Her breast displays two silver fountains bright,
The Spheres her voice, her grace the Graces three,
Her body is the Saint that I adore,
Her smiles and favors sweet as honey be,
Her feet fair Thetis praiseth evermore.
But ah the worst and last is yet behind,
For of a Gryphon she doth bear the mind."
(Bartholomew Griffin, *Fidessa*, XXXIX)

Effiguration. Elaborate description of an object or event, but not of a person.

Egressio (e GRESS i o) — **Digression.**

Eidolopoeia (eid o lo POE i a; G. "formation of [often mental] images"). Presenting a dead person as speaking, or the speech thus assigned.

Elevatio (el e VA ti o) — **Diasyrmus.**

Ellipsis (el LIP sis; G. "to fall short; leave out"); alt. sp. **Eclip-**

sis — **Brachylogia; Default.** *See also* **Praegnans Constructio.**
Omission of a word easily understood: "And he to England
shall along with you" (*Hamlet*, III, iii).

Elocutio (el o CU ti o; L. "utterance, expression") — **Lexis.**
See also **Phrasis.** The Latin term for **Style,** *q.v.,* the third of the
five parts of rhetoric.

Emblem (G. "an insertion"). Representation that stands for or
suggests something else; symbol; a motto, sometimes accompanied by a picture; sometimes, a symbolic picture or design by
itself.

Emphasis — Reinforcer. Rhet. and log.: Stress of language in
such a way as to imply more than is actually stated. *See also*
Significatio.

> "My man is become a lord of late, whereby is signified,
> that the same servant is proud, stout, and disobedient."
> (Peacham)

Enallage (EN al lage; G. "interchange") — **Changeling; Exchange.** Substitution of one case, person, gender, number, tense,
mood, part of speech, for another. *See also* **Alleotheta; Anthimeria.**

> "*Gender*: It is a wicked daughter that despises his
> mother. Wind is loud, she bloweth cold. *Person*: Here
> he is, what have you to say for him? *for* Here I am."
> (Peacham)

Enantiosis (en an ti o sis; G. "opposition").
1. **Irony.**
2. **Contrarium.**

Enargia (en ar GI a; G. "vividness, distinctness"). Vivid description. Overlaps with **Energia.** One can, if it is expedient, distinguish the purposeful movement of energia from the distinctness
of enargia. Both terms, when used in discussions of seventeenth-
century English prose style, sometimes overlap and/or coincide
with the "point" of the **Pointed Style,** *q.v.*

Encomium (G. "eulogy"); alt. sp. **Ecomium — Commendatio.**
Praise of a person or thing by extolling inherent qualities. *See also*
Comprobatio; Eulogia.

Energia (en er GI a; G. "activity;" rhet. "vigor of style") —
Ecphrasis; Hypotyposis; Descriptio; Informatio; Diatyposis (1).
1. Clear, lucid, vivid description.
2. Generic term that includes: **Ethopoeia; Characterismus;
Prosopographia; Prosopopoeia; Mimesis; Dialogismus; Pragma-**

tographia; **Topographia; Topothesia; Icon; Pathopoeia; Sermocinatio.** *See also* **Enargia.**

Enigma (G. "allusive or obscure speech"); alt. sp. **Aenigma.** A
riddle. *See also* **Noema; Riddle; Schematismus.**

Enthymeme (EN thy meme; G. "thought, piece of reasoning") —
Aggressio; Epicheireme; Commentatio; Commentum.

1. Maintaining the truth of a proposition from the assumed
   truth of its contrary:
   "If it be great praise to please good men,
      Surely to please evil men it is a great shame."
                           (Sherry)

2. Log.: abridged syllogism, one of the terms being omitted
   as understood.

3. Rhet.: Aristotle uses the term to mean a "syllogism" in
   which the premises are only generally true, a rhetorical
   syllogism. If they are absolutely true (scientifically proved)
   the proper term is syllogism. Thinking that Aristotle meant
   enthymeme to refer to the shortened form of any syllogism, later theorists called the rhetorical syllogism in full
   form **Epicheireme.** (See Quintilian, V, xiv, 14) Prevailing
   usage today seems to make enthymeme equivalent to rhetorical syllogism or shortened syllogism of any sort, and to
   ignore epicheireme. The enthymeme and the example were,
   for Aristotle, the two fundamental logical tools of rhetoric.
   See also **Aetiologia.**

Entrance — Exordium.

Enumeratio (e num er A ti o).

1. Division of subject into adjuncts, cause into effects, ante-
   cedent into consequents. *See also* **Digestion; Eutrepismus:**
   "How do I love thee? Let me count the ways.
   I love thee to the depth and breadth and height
   My soul can reach, when feeling out of sight
   For the ends of Being and ideal Grace.
   I love thee to the level of everyday's
   Most quiet need, by sun and candlelight.
   I love thee freely, as men strive for Right;
   I love thee purely, as they turn from Praise.
   I love thee with the passion put to use
   In my old griefs, and with my childhood's faith.
   I love thee with a love I seemed to lose
   With my lost saints, — I love thee with the breath,

> Smiles, tears, of all my life! — and, if God choose,
> I shall but love thee better after death."
>
> (Elizabeth Barrett Browning)

2. A summary or recapitulation, intended to refresh the hearer's memory. **Anacephalaeosis.**

Epagoge (EP a go ge; G. "to bring in or forward") — **Inductio.** An inductive argument, or a series of them: "a form of argument which leads the person with whom one is arguing to give assent to certain undisputed facts: through this assent it wins his approval of a doubtful proposition because this resembles the facts to which he has assented." The argument Cicero uses as illustration:

> ". . . in a dialogue by Aeschines Socraticus Socrates reveals that Aspasia reasoned thus with Xenophon's wife and with Xenophon himself: 'Please tell me, madam, if your neighbor had a better gold ornament than you have, would you prefer that one or your own?' 'That one,' she replied. 'Now, if she had dresses and other feminine finery more expensive than you have, would you prefer yours or hers?' 'Hers, of course,' she replied. 'Well, now, if she had a better husband than you have, would you prefer your husband or hers?' "

> (*De Inventione*, I, xxxi, 51)

Epanadiplosis (e pan a di PLO sis; G. "doubling") — **Epanalepsis.**

Epanalepsis (ep a na LEP sis; G. "resumption, repetition") — **Epanadiplosis; Repetitio; Slowe Returne; Eccho Sounde.** Repetition at the end of a clause or sentence of the word with which it began: "I might, unhappy word, O me, I might" (Sidney, *Astrophil and Stella*, XXXIII).

Epanaphora (ep a NAPH o ra; G. "carrying back"). Intensive **Anaphora.**

Epanodos (ep A no dos; G. "return, recapitulation; fuller statement of a point").

1. **Prolepsis; Regressio; Retire.** A general statement is expanded by discussing it part by part, with the further qualification that the terms used in the summary are specifically repeated in the fuller discussion that follows:
   "Of those he chose out two, the falsest twoo,

And fittest for to forge true-seeming lyes;
The one of them he gaue a message too,
The other by him selfe staide other worke to doo."
(Spenser, *Faerie Queene*, I, i, 38)

2. **Ploce.**

Epanorthosis (e pan or THO sis; G. "setting straight"). **Correctio** (1).

Epecphonesis (ep ec pho NE sis) — **Ecphonesis.**

Epembasis (e PEM ba sis; G. "attack, advance") — **Anaphora.**

Epenthesis (e PEN the sis; G. "to place in addition") — **Interpositio** (2). Addition of a letter, sound, or syllable to the middle of a word: "Lie blist'ring fore the visitating sun" (*Two Noble Kinsmen*, I, i).

Epergesis (ep ER ge sis) — **Appositio.** Apposition; placing two nouns together without a verb, the second defining the first.

Epexegesis (e pex e GE sis; G. "to explain in addition") — **Explanatio.** Adding words or phrases to further clarify or specify a statement already made: "For I know that in me, (that is, in my flesh), dwelleth no good thing" (Romans 7:18).

Epexergasia — **Exergasia.**

Epezeugmenon (ep e ZEUG men on; G. "joined").

1. **Zeugma.**
2. Minor premise of a disjunctive syllogism.

Ephodos (EPH o dos; G. "[means of] approach"). The "Subtle Approach"; one of the two kinds of openings or introductions. The other is **Prooemium,** *q v,* or Direct Opening.

Epicertomesis (ep i cer to ME sis; G. "sarcasm, taunt") — **Chleuasmos.**

Epicheireme (ep i chei REME; G. "an attempt") — **Aggressio.** *See also* **Enthymeme.**

Epicrisis (e PIC ri sis; G. "determination; discrimination") — **Ajudicatio.** The speaker quotes a passage and comments on it: you have been told. . . . I say to you however. . . .

Epidiorthosis (ep i di or THO sis) — **Correctio** (1).

Epilogue (G. "to speak in addition").

1. Inferring what will follow from what has been spoken or done before:

"Did you perceive
He did solicit you in free contempt
When he did need your loves, and do you think

> That his contempt shall not be bruising to you,
> When he hath power to crush?"
>
> (*Coriolanus*, II, iii)

2. **Conclusion.**

Epimone (e PI mo ne; G. "tarrying, delay") — **Perseverentia; Love Burden.** Frequent repetition of a phrase or question; dwelling on a point:

> "So downe he fell, and forth his life did breath,
>   That vanisht into smoke and cloudes swift;
>   So downe he fell, that th'earth him vnderneath
>   Did grone, as feeble so great load to lift;
>   So downe he fell, as an huge rockie clift,
>   Whose false foundation waues haue washt away,
>   With dreadfull poyse is from the mauneland rift,
>   And rolling downe, great Neptune doth dismay;
> So downe he fell, and like an heaped mountaine lay."
>
> (Spenser, *Faerie Queene*, I, xi, 54)

Epiphonema (ep i pho NEM a; G. "witty saying; phrase added by way of ornament or as a finishing touch") — **Acclamatio; Surclose; Consenting Close;** alt. sp. **Epithoncma.** Striking epigrammatic or sententious utterance to summarize and conclude a passage, poem, or speech:

> "This said, adowne he looked to the ground,
>   To haue returned, but dazed were his eyne,
>   Through passing brightnesse, which did quite confound
>   His feeble sence, and too exceeding shyne.
> So darke are earthly things compared to things diuine."
>
> (Spenser, *Faerie Queene*, I, x, 67)

Epiphonesis (ep i pho NE sis; G. "acclamation") — **Ecphonesis.**

Epiphora (e PIPH o ra; G. "a bringing to or upon") — **Antistrophe** (1); **Epistrophe** (1). Repetition of a word or phrase at the end of several (usually successive) clauses, sentences, or verses: opposite of **Anaphora:** Peacham cites I Corinthians 13:11: "When I was a child, I spake as a child, I understood as a child, I thought as a child: but when I became a man, I put away childish things."

Epiplexis (ep i PLEX is; G. "rebuke") — **Percontatio; Epitimesis.** Asking questions in order to reproach or upbraid, rather than to elicit information, as Cicero against Catiline: "How long will you abuse our sufferance? How long will this rage and madness of yours go about to deceive us?"

Epiploce (ep i PLO ce; G. "plaiting together") — **Ploce.** The etymology would seem to imply a series in some particular (perhaps climactic) order.

Epistrophe (e PIS tro phe; G. "turning away").

1. Rhet. **Antistrophe** (1); **Epiphora.** Repetition of a closing word or words at the end of several clauses, sentences, or verses: "And all the night he did nothing but weep Philoclea, sigh Philoclea, and cry out Philoclea" (Sidney, *New Arcadia*, III).

2. Log.: conversion of a proposition.

Epitheton (e PITH e ton; G. "attributed"); alt. sp. **Epithet** — **Attribution; Qualifier.** Qualifying the subject with an appropriate adjective; an adjective that frequently or habitually accompanies a certain noun:

> "On thother side, in one consort, there sate
> Cruell Revenge, and rancorous Despight,
> Disloyall Treason, and hart-burning Hate."
> (Spenser, *Faerie Queene*, II, vii, 22)

Epitimesis (ep i ti ME sis; G. "rebuke").

1. **Epiplexis.**

2. **Correctio** (2).

Epitrochasmus (ep i tro CHAS mus; G. "run lightly over, treat briefly") — **Percursio.** A swift movement from one statement to the other; rapid touching on many different points. (**Concervatio** is the opposite figure.)

> "All Kings, and all their favorites,
> All glory of honours, beauties, wits,
> The sun itself, which makes times, as they pass,
> Is elder by a year, now, than it was
> When thou and I first one another saw:
> All other things, to their destruction draw,
> Only our love hath no decay;
> This, no tomorrow hath, nor yesterday,
> Running, it never runs from us away,
> But truly keeps his first, last, everlasting day."
> (Donne, *The Anniversary*)

Epitrope (e PI tro pe; G. "to give up, yield"). — **Confessio.**

1. Permission or submission to an opponent or disputant, either earnest or, as when Cleopatra speaks to Antony, ironical:

> "Nay, pray you seek no colour for your going,

But bid farewell, and go. When you su'd staying,
Then was the time for words. No going then!
Eternity was in our lips and eyes."

(I, iii)

2. **Anacoenosis.**

Epizeuxis (ep i ZEUX is; G. "fastening upon") — **Doublet; Geminatio; Cuckowspell; Underlay.** Emphatic repetition of a word with no other words between: "O horror, horror, horror!" *See also* **Palilogia** (2).

Erotema — Erotesis.

Erotesis (er o TE sis; G. "a questioning") — **Interrogatio; Questioner.** Rhetorical question implying strong affirmation or denial, as when Laertes laments Ophelia's madness:

"O heavens! is't possible a young maid's wits
Should be as mortal as an old man's life?"

(*Hamlet*, IV, v)

See also **Hypophora; Ratiocinatio; Epiplexis.**

Ethopoeia (eth o PEE a; G. "delineation of character"); alt. sp. **Aetopoeia.**
1. Type of **Energia:** description of natural propensities, manners, affections, virtues, and vices in order to flatter or reproach; character portrayal generally.
2. Putting oneself in the place of another, so as to both understand and express his feelings more vividly, i.e., thinking like a jewel thief, if you are defending one. The Greek orator Lysias was supposed to be the first to develop this technique fully; it does not seem too far removed from "method" acting, or indeed from naturalistic acting of any sort. The term might be used, though to my knowledge it never has been, to describe the "acting" of a character in a play-within-a-play, Falstaff "playing" the King in *I Henry IV*, for example.

See also **Dialogismus.**

Ethos (E thos; G. "disposition, character"). *See* **Pathos.**

Etiologia — Aetiologia.

Eucharistia (eu char IS ti a; G. "a thanksgiving"); alt. sp. **Eucharista — Gratiarum Actio.** Giving thanks; prayer of thanksgiving.

Euche (EU che; G. "prayer, vow") — **Votum.** *See also* **Eustathia.**
1. Vow or oath to keep a promise.
2. Prayer for evil; curse.

Eulogia (eu LO gi a; G. "praise, blessing") — **Benedictio.** Commending or blessing a person or thing. *See also* **Comprobatio; Encomium.**

"And he opened his mouth, and taught them, saying,
Blessed are the poor in spirit: for theirs is the kingdom
of heaven.
Blessed are they that mourn: for they shall be comforted.
Blessed are the meek, for they shall inherit the earth."
(Matt. 5:2–5)

Euphemismus (eu phe MIS mus; G. "to speak fair") — **Curry Favell; Soother.**
1. Rhet.: Prognostication of good; opposite of **Ominatio.**
2. Circumlocution to palliate something unpleasant; "pass away" for "die."

Euphuism. The elaborately patterned prose style of John Lyly's prose romance *Euphues* (1579). It emphasizes the figures of words that create balance, and makes frequent use of antithesis, paradox, repetitive patterns with single words, sound-plays of various sorts, amplification of all sorts, unremitting use of the sententia and especially the "unnatural natural history" or simile from traditional natural history. Euphuism has now come to mean any highly figured, Asiatic style. Lyly's style has been studied largely to be deplored. The central charge has been that it is wholly ornamental, a bag of superficial verbal tricks which exists for its own sake rather than to create meaning, as modern critics customarily expect highly figurative language to justify itself by doing. Recently this verdict has undergone some modification, however. G. K. Hunter (*John Lyly: The Humanist as Courtier*) has pointed out how Lyly's patterned prose brought a new discipline and symmetry to the resources of English prose. Jonas Barish ("The Prose Style of John Lyly") has tried to show how some of the figures are used, what particular purposes Lyly had in mind. And several scholars have tried to call attention to the fictional, often highly dramatic, context of much Elizabethan rhetorical prose. Not what figures are used so much as how they are used, would seem to be the next lesson euphuistic prose has to teach us. In this connection one might cite Northrop Frye's clever observation on the self-consciousness of the euphuistic style: "Euphuism . . . is easy to parody, but in euphuism itself there is a curious quality that is really a kind of self-parody. Its ingenuity makes it witty, and the wit may be conscious or, at times, unconscious" (*The Well-Tempered Critic*, pp. 64–65).

In any event, Euphuism must remain the rhetorical prose style par excellence, and the strongest warning that a rhetorical style in a fictional matrix needs a fuller range of critical equipment than the rhetorical theorist by himself can provide. An example from *Euphues*:

> "True it is Philautus that he which toucheth the nettle tenderly, is soonest stung, that the fly which playeth with the fire is singed in the flame, that he that dallieth with women is drawn to his woe. And as the adamant draweth the heavy iron, the harp the fleet dolphin, so beauty allureth the chaste mind to live, & the wisest wit to lust: The example whereof I would it were no less profitable than the experience to me is like to be perilous. The vine watered with wine is soon withered, the blossom in the fattest ground is quickly blasted, the goat the fatter she is the less fertile she is; yea, man the more witty he is the less happy he is."

See **Asiatismus.**

Eustathia (eu stath I a; G. "stability, tranquillity") — **Constantia.** Pledge of constancy. *See also* **Euche.**

> "For certes, fresshe wommanliche wif,
>   This dar I saye, that trouthe and diligence,
>   That shal ye finden in me al my lif;
>   N'I wol nat, certain, breke youre defence:
>   And if I do, present or in absence,
>   For love of God, lat slee me with the deede,
>   If that it like unto youre wommanhede."
>   (*Troilus and Criseide*, III)

Eutrepismus (eu tre PIS mus; G. "to make ready") — **Ordinatio.** Dividing or ordering a subject into a number of parts. *See* **Enumeratio.**

Even. Puttenham's term for **Parison.** *See* **Isocolon.**

Exacerbatio (ex a cer BA ti o; L. "exasperation") — **Sarcasmus.**

Exadversio (ex ad VER si o; L. "opposition") — **Litotes.**

Excessus (ex CESS us) — **Digression.**

Exchange. Puttenham's term for **Enallage.**

Exclamatio (ex cla MA ti o) — **Ecphonesis.**

Excogitata (ex co gi TA ta; L. "to find out by thinking") — **Pareuresis.**

Excursus (ex CURS us) — **Digression.**
Excusatio (ex cu SA ti o) — **Pareuresis.**
Excuse — **Dicaeologia.**
Execratio (ex e CRA ti o) — **Ara.**
Exemplum (ex EM plum; L. "a sample") — **Paradigma.** An example cited, either true or feigned; illustrative story. *See also* **Paradiegesis.**

"Such first was *Bacchus*, that with furious might
　　All th'East before vntam'd did ouerronne,
　　And wrong repressed, and establisht right,
　　Which lawlesse men had formerly fordonne.
　　There Iustice first her princely rule begonne.
　　Next *Hercules* his like ensample shewed,
　　Who all the West with equall conquest wonne,
　　And monstrous tyrants with his club subdewed;
The club of Iustice dread, with kingly powre endewed."
　　　　　　　　　　(Spenser, *Faerie Queene*, V, i, 2)

Exergasia (ex er GA si a; G. "working out"); alt. sp. **Exargasia** — **Expolitio; Epexergasia; Gorgious.** Repeating the same thought in many figures:

"I take thy hand — this hand,
　As soft as dove's down and as white as it,
　Or Ethiopian's tooth, or the fann'd snow that's bolted
　By the northern blasts twice o'er."
　　　　　　　　　　(*Winter's Tale*, IV, iv)

Exgressus (ex GRESS us) — **Digression.**
Exordium (ex OR di um; L. "beginning") — **Entrance; Prooemium.** The first part of the seven-part classical oration. It caught the audience's interest while introducing the subject. It was sometimes divided into the direct (*principium*) and the indirect (*insinuatio*). See the full list of parts in 2.4.
Expeditio (ex pe DI ti o; L. lit. "to untangle the feet from a snare") — **Speedie Dispatcher.** Rejection of all but one of various alternatives. *See also* **Apophasis.**

"Seeing that this land was mine, thou must needs show
　that either thou didst possess it being void, or made it
　thine by use, or purchase, or else that it came to thee
　by inheritance: Thou couldst not possess it void
　when I was in possession; also thou canst not make it
　thine by use nor custom. Thou hast no deed to evidence thy purchase of it; I being alive it could not

descend upon thee by inheritance: it follows then that thou wouldst put me from mine own land, before I be dead."

(Smith)

Experientia (ex per i EN ti a) — **Apodixis.**
Explanatio (ex pla NA ti o) — **Epexegesis.**
Explicatio (ex pli CA ti o) — **Exposition.**
Expolitio (ex po LI ti o; L. "polishing, adorning, embellishing") — **Exergasia.**
Exposition (L. "putting forth, setting forth") — **Definitio; Explicatio.** The third part of the seven-part classical oration. It defines terms and opens issues to be proved.
Exprobatio (ex pro BA ti o) — **Onedismus** (1).
Extension. Roughly, denotation of a term; log.: all the subclasses of a given class.
Extenuatio (ex ten u A ti o). Representing a thing or an event as less than it is: "I had a scrape with the police" for "I spent 10 years in jail." *See* **Litotes.**
Exuperatio (ex u per A ti o) — **Hyperbole.**
Exuscitatio (ex u sci TA ti o; L. "awakening, arousing"). Emotional utterance that moves hearers to like feeling:

"Doth it not abhor you to hear and understand of a rabble of so great and unaccustomed lewdness, a man every way so vile, to go thus freely unpunished?"

(Day)

Fable (L. "discourse, narrative, story") — **Apologue.** A short allegorical story that points a lesson or moral; the characters are frequently animals.
Fallacy (Logical). Two forms:
1. Formal — violates rules of syllogism.
2. Informal or material.
    a. Relevance
        1) *Argumentum ad Baculum* (appeal to force).
        2) *Argumentum ad Hominem* (disparage the character of the speaker, instead of attacking his arguments).
        3) *Argumentum ad Ignorantiam* (argue that a proposition is true because it has never been proved false).
        4) *Argumentum ad Misericordium* (appeal to pity).

5) *Argumentum ad Populum* (play on the feelings of the audience).

6) *Argumentum ad Verecundiam* (appeal to traditional values).

7) Converse Accident (fallacious generalization on the basis of unrepresentative sample).

8) *Post hoc, propter hoc* (because A occurs before B, A is the cause of B: confusion of temporal and causal sequence).

9) *Petitio Principii* (assuming as a premise the conclusion to be proved).

10) Rigged Question (the terms of the question require admission as part of *any* answer: Have you stopped beating your wife?).

11) *Ignoratio Elenchi* (a conclusion irrelevant to the argument that attempts to prove it).

  b. Ambiguity

1) Equivocation (deliberate confusion of two or more meanings of a word).

2) Amphiboly (argument from ambiguous premise).

3) Accent (deliberate change of stress or emphasis to change meaning).

4) Composition (deliberately taking a part for the whole).

5) Division (deliberately taking the whole for a part).

6) 4 and 5 together are sometimes called *Secundum Quid.*

False Semblant. Puttenham's term for **Allegory.**

Far-Fet. Puttenham's term for **Metalepsis.**

Fictio (FIC ti o; L. "invention"). Attributing reasonable actions and speech to unreasonable creatures:

"With how sad steps, ô Moone, thou climb'st the skies,
  How silently, and with how wanne a face,
  What, may it be that even in heav'nly place
That busie archer his sharpe arrowes tries?
Sure, if that long with *Love* acquainted eyes
  Can judge of *Love*, thou feel'st a Lover's case;
  I reade it in thy lookes, thy languisht grace,
To me that feele the like, thy state descries."
                (Sidney, *Astrophil and Stella*, XXXI)

Figure. A general term for any striking or unusual configuration of words or phrases, any departure from normal usage. *See* **Trope;** *also* 2.5.3.

Fleering Frumpe. Puttenham's term for **Mycterismus.**

Flitting Figure. Puttenham's term for **Metastasis.**

Fonde Affectation. Puttenham's term for **Cacozelia.**

Formulae. *See* **Ars Dictaminis.**

Forrein Speech. Puttenham's term for **Barbarismus.**

Foule Speech. Puttenham's term for **Cacemphaton.**

Frequentatio (fre quen TA ti o; L. "crowding together"). **Synathroesmus.**

Geminatio (ge mi NA ti o; L. "doubling") — **Epizeuxis.**

Geographia (ge o GRAPH i a). Description of the earth. *See also* **Prosopographia; Topographia; Chorographia; Chronographia; Hydrographia; Anemographia; Dendrographia.**

> "Earth, ocean, air, beloved brotherhood!
> If our great Mother has imbued my soul
> With aught of natural piety to feel
> Your love, and recompense the boon with mine;
> If dewy morn, and odorous noon, and even,
> With sunset and its gorgeous ministers,
> And solemn midnight's tingling silentness;
> If autumn's hollow sighs in the sere wood,
> And winter robing with pure snow and crowns
> Of starry ice the grey grass and bare boughs;
> If spring's voluptuous pantings when she breathes
> Her first sweet kisses, have been dear to me;
> If no bright bird, insect, or gentle beast
> I consciously have injured, but still loved
> And cherished these my kindred; then forgive
> This boast, beloved brethren, and withdraw
> No portion of your wonted favour now!"
>
> (Shelley, *Alastor*)

Gnome ([g]NOME; G. "thought, judgment, opinion") — **Proverb,** *q.v. See* **Paroemia.** *See also* **Apothegm; Maxim; Sententia; Aphorism; Adage.** A short pithy statement of a general truth: "All change is perillous, and all chaunce vnsound" (Spenser, *Faerie Queene*, V, ii, 36).

Gorgious. Puttenham's term for **Exergasia.**

Graciosa Nugatio (grac i o sa   nu GAT i o; L. "pleasant nonsense or jesting") — **Charientismus.**

Gradatio (gra DAT i o) — **Climax.**

Graecismus (grae CIS mus; f. L. *Graecus*: "Greek"). Use of Greek idiom, grammatical, or orthographical feature in writing or speaking English.

Gratiarum Actio (gra ti AR um   AC ti o) — **Eucharistia.**

Heaping Figure. Puttenham's term for **Synathroesmus.**

Hebraism. Use of Hebrew idiom, grammatical or orthographical feature, in writing or speaking another language.

Hendiadys (hen DY a dis; G. "one by means of two"); alt. sp. **Hendiasys — Twinnes.** Expression of an idea by two nouns connected by "and" instead of a noun and its qualifier: "by length of time and siege" for "by a long siege." Peacham, ignoring the derivation of the term, defines it as the substituting, for an adjective, of a substantive with the same meaning: "a man of great wisdom" for "a wise man." This redefinition would make it a kind of **Anthimeria**, *q.v.*

Heterogenium (het er o GE ni um; G. "of a different kind"). Irrelevant answer to distract attention from a difficult point: "I ask you of cheese, you answer me of chalk" (Fenner).

Heuresis (HEUR e sis; G. "discovery, invention") — **Invention.**

Hiatus (hi AT us; L. "gaping, gap, opening"). The frequent harsh collision of vowels; two vowel sounds not separated by a consonant. Opposite of elision.

Hirmus (HIR mus; G. "series, sequence"); alt. sp. **Heirmos; Hyrmos; Irmus.** What Puttenham calls the "**Long Loose,**" a **Periodic Sentence**, *q.v.*, in which the sense is suspended through a series of markedly parallel elements. Puttenham quotes Wyatt.

> "If waker care, if sudden pale color:
> If many sighs, with little speech to plain:
> Now joy, now woe: if they may cheer disdain
> For hope of small, if much to fear therefore,
> To haste, or slack: my pace to less, or more:
> Be sign of love: then do I love again."

Homiologia (hom i o LO gi a; G. "uniformity of style"). The etymologically correct spelling should be "homoiologia," of course.

1. Tedious, redundant style:

> "POLONIUS: Madam, I swear I use no art at all.
> That he is mad, 'tis true: 'tis true 'tis pity;
> And pity 'tis 'tis true: a foolish figure;
> But farewell it, for I will use no art.

Mad let us grant him, then: and now remains
That we find out the cause of this effect,
Or rather say, the cause of this defect,
For this effect defective comes by cause:
Thus it remains and the remainder thus."

(Hamlet, II, ii)

See also **Macrology; Poiciologia.**
   2. Uniform style.
Homoeoprophoron (hom oe o PRO phor on; G. "similar in pronunciation") — **Alliteration.**
Homoeosis (hom oe o sis; G. "likeness, resemblance"); alt. sp.
Omiosis. General figure of similitude the types of which are
Icon; Fable; Paradigma; Parable.
Homoioptoton (hom oi op TO ton; G. "in a like case, with a
similar inflexion"); alt. sp. **Homoeoptoton — Similiter Cadens**
(1); **Simile Casibus.** In classical rhetorical theory, the use of
various words, in a sentence or verse, with similar case endings;
lacking a real series of inflections, English uses the term loosely,
often making it synonymous with **Homoioteleuton,** often making
it mean simply rhyme. So Wilson, in the *Arte of Rhetorique*,
gives this example: "By great travail is gotten much avail, by
earnest affection men learn discretion."
For a fuller discussion, see the following entry.
Homoioteleuton (hom oi o te LEU ton; G. "like ending"); alt. sp.
**Homoeuteleuton — Similiter Desinens; Simile Determinatione;
Like Loose.** The confusion of this term with **Homoioptoton**
above is partly a result of the adaption of the pair of terms from
an inflected to an uninflected language, partly a result of confusion in classical theory itself.
   Quintilian (IX, iii, 77–80) distinguishes between the two prin-
cipally by the size of the elements that terminate alike. Homoioteleuton he defines: "when clauses conclude alike, the same
syllables being placed at the end of each . . . correspondence
in the ending of two or more sentences. . . ." The similarity
could come, presumably, from similar terminations of any sort,
not just similar inflections. In terms of English use, then, it would
mean simply rhymed verses. **Homoioptoton**, on the other hand,
he defines as the "use of similar cases." He then qualifies this in a
special way:
      "But this name, though it implies a certain similarity,
      does not necessarily involve identity in termination,

since it means no more than similarity of case, irrespective of the fact that words may be differently declined, and does not always occur at the end of a sentence; the correspondence may occur at the beginning, middle, or end of clauses, or may be varied so that the middle of one clause corresponds with the beginning of another and the end with the middle: in fact, any arrangement of correspondences is permissible."

Such a qualification seems at odds with its general meaning in classical theory. The point of using, or avoiding, similar endings depended — as a theoretical issue — on the sound similarity. (Thus a writer might find *magnarum terrarum* an inelegant jingle and choose an adjective of another declension, *grandium*, say, to avoid the sound similarity. Or, of course, he might reverse the process in order to obtain the resemblance intentionally. As a general prose rule, variation by use of an adjective of another declension was thought desirable.)

The author of *Rhetorica ad Herennium* (IV, xx, 28) distinguishes the two terms on the basis of type of termination. "The figure called Homoeoptoton occurs when in the same period two or more words appear in the same case, and with like terminations. . . ." And in all the examples that he adduces, the inflections are *identical*, not simply properly agreeing, as Quintilian has it. "Homoeoteleuton occurs when the word endings are similar, although the words are indeclinable." He cites as example: "*Turpiter audes facere, nequiter studes disere*; You dare to act dishonorably, you strive to talk despicably. . . ." He concludes: "These two figures, of which one depends on like word endings and the other on like case endings, are very much of a piece."

The Tudor theorists seem to have followed the *Ad Herennium*. Puttenham gives a string of "ly" adverbs as exemplifying homoioteleuton. Thus it is like ending in uninflected words, or rhyme. Wilson identifies homoioptoton as similar inflections. Yet there was confusion even then, and certainly has been since, between the two terms as used in English rhetorical theory. Since the issue of inflections is not crucial in English, perhaps it might be better to use homoioptoton to mean similar termination of a pair or series of words within a sentence or verse, homoioteleuton to mean a similar closing of several sentences or verses.

Horismus (ho RIS mus; G. "marking out by boundaries, limitation") — **Definitio; Definer by Difference.** A brief definition, often antithetical: "He has a strong voice but not a pleasing one."

Humilatio (hu mi LA ti o) — **Tapinosis.**

Hydrographia (hy dro GRAPH i a). Description of water. *See also* **Prosopographia; Topographia; Chorographia; Chronographia; Geographia; Anemographia; Dendrographia.**

Hypallage (hy PAL la ge; G. "interchange, exchange") — **Changeling.**

1. Awkward or humorous changing of agreement or application of words, as with Bottom:

> "I see a voice. Now will I to the chink,
>   To spy and I can hear my Thisby's face."
>   (*Midsummer Night's Dream*, V, i)

2. **Metonymy.**
3. Gram.: "a change in the relation of words by which a word, instead of agreeing with the case it logically qualifies, is made to agree grammatically with another case" (Smythe, *Greek Grammar*, p. 678).
4. Often used to describe a deliberately misapplied epithet.

Hyperbaton (hy PER ba ton; G. "going beyond; [of words] transposed").

1. **Caresyntheton; Transgressio; Cacosyntheton; Transcensio; Transiectio; Trespasser.** A generic figure of various forms of departure from ordinary word order including **Anastrophe; Tmesis; Hysteron Proteron; Hypallage; Hysterologia; Parenthesis; Epergesis.**
2. Separation of words usually belonging together. Churchill's humorous illustration of "good usage" is an example: "This is the kind of impertinence up with which I will not put." Quintilian (VIII, vi, 65) offers an orthodox Latin example, in which *partes* is stressed by terminal position: "animadverti, iudices, omnem accusatoris orationem in duas divisam esse partes." ("I noted, gentlemen, that the speech of the accuser was divided into two parts.")

Hyperbole (hy PER bo le; G. "excess, exaggeration") — **Superlatio; Loud Lyer; Overreacher.** Exaggerated or extravagant terms used for emphasis and not intended to be understood literally; self-conscious exaggeration:

> "For instance, of a Lion;

He roared so loud, and looked so wondrous grim,
His very shadow durst not follow him."
(Pope, *Peri Bathous*)

Hyperzeugma (hy per ZEUG ma). Opposite of **Zeugma.** Each phrase has its own verb. Churchill's speech uses both verbs and prepositions:

"We shall not flag or fail. We shall fight in France, we shall fight on the seas and oceans, we shall fight with growing confidence and growing strength in the air, we shall defend our island, whatever the cost may be, we shall fight on the landing grounds, we shall fight in the fields and in the streets, we shall fight in the hills; we shall never surrender."

Hypocrisis (hy POC ri sis; G. "reply; [orator's] delivery"). Exaggerating an opponent's gestures or speech habits in order to mock him.

Hypodiastole (hy po di AS to le) — **Comma.** A brief pause in reading or speaking.

Hypophora (hy PO phor a) — **Anthypophora; Antiphora; Apocrisis; Subjectio.** Raising questions and answering them, as in Falstaff's catechism on honor:

"What is honour? a word. What is that word, honour; Air. A trim reckoning! Who hath it? He that dies o' Wednesday. Doth he feel it? No. Doth he hear it? No. . . ."
(*I Henry IV*, V, i)

Hypotaxis (hy po TAX is; G. "subjection"). An arrangement of clauses or phrases in a dependent or subordinate relationship. Opposite of **Parataxis.**

"Antiquity held too light thoughts from objects of morality, while some drew provocatives of mirth from anatomies, and jugglers showed tricks with skeletons, when fiddlers made not so pleasant mirth as fencers, and men could sit with quiet stomachs while hanging was played before them."
(Sir Thomas Browne, *Hydriotaphia*, chap. 3)

Hypothesis (G. "the subject under discussion"). One of the two categories into which the Greek rhetorician Hermagoras of Temnos divided the subjects of rhetoric. It was a specific subject, concerned with individual people, places, etc. For example, "Is

Hamlet responsible for Polonius' death?" The Latin term was *causa*. The opposite category was **Thesis.**

Hypothetical (or Conditional) Propositions. A hypothetical proposition is composed of an "if" clause, called the antecedent, and a "then" clause, called the consequent: "If John has joined the army, then he is a fool."

Hypothetical Syllogism. A syllogism that contains only **Hypothetical Propositions,** *q.v.,* is called a pure hypothetical syllogism. If it also contains **Categorical Propositions,** *q.v.,* it is a mixed hypothetical syllogism.

Hypotyposis (hy po ty PO sis; G. "sketch, outline, pattern").
   1. **Energia; Counterfait Representation.**
   2. Mimicry of acts only, not manners or feelings. *See* **Mimesis; Pragmatographia.**

Hypozeugma (hy po ZEUG ma; G. "bring under the yoke") — **Rerewarder.** Use of one verb in the last clause of a sentence which is understood in the others: "Hours, days, weeks, months, and years do pass away" (Sherry).
See also **Zeugma.**

Hypozeuxis (hy po ZEUX is) — **Substitute.** Every clause in a sentence has its own subject and verb:
> "Madam, the guests are come, supper serv'd up, you call'd, my young lady ask'd for, the nurse curs'd in the pantry, and everything in extremity."
>   (*Romeo and Juliet,* I, iii)

Hysterologia (hys ter o LO gi a). Form of **Hyperbaton.**
   1. A phrase is interposed between a preposition and its object: "I ran after with as much speed as I could, the thief that had undone me" (Peacham).
   2. Sherry makes the term mean **Hysteron Proteron**: "When that is done afterwards, is set in speaking in the former place, as: pluck off my boots and spurs." He gives **Prepostera Locutio** as the Latin equivalent.

Hysteron Proteron (HYS ter on   PRO te ron; G. "the latter [put as] the former") — **Preposterous.** Form of **Hyperbaton:** syntax or sense out of normal logical or temporal order:
> "ENOBARBUS: Th'Antoniad, the Egyptian admiral,
>   With all their sixty, fly and turn the
>   rudder."
>   (*Antony and Cleopatra,* III, x)

See also **Anastrophe.**

Icon (I con; G. "likeness, image, portrait"); alt. sp. **Eicon** — **Resemblance by Imagerie.** Form of homoeosis: painting resemblance by imagery, as when Richard II describes himself:

"Down, down I come, like glist'ring Phaeton,
Wanting the manage of unruly jades."

(III, iii)

See also **Simile, Image.**

Ignoratio Elenchi (ig no RA ti o   e LEN chi; L. "ignorance of confutation"). Irrelevant conclusion: *See* **Fallacy (Logical);** *also* 2.3.5.

Illusio (il LU si o; L. "mocking, jeering") — **Irony.**

Illustratio (il lu STRA ti o); alt. sp. **Inlustratio.** Vivid representation.

Image. (L. "imitation, copy, likeness") — **Imago.** A thing that represents something else; a symbol, emblem, representation. The term "imagery," as it is used today in literary criticism, was not part of the traditional rhetorical nomenclature. The pictorial (visual image-making) part of its meaning was expressed by the various subdivisions of **Energia;** the more common of its present meanings, figurative expression generally, was divided up into a long list of figures — not all of them tropes, of course. *See also* **Icon.**

Imminutio (im mi NU ti o) — **Meiosis.**

Impartener. Puttenham's term for **Anacoenosis.**

Impossibilia (im pos si BIL i a) — **Adynata.**

Imprecatio (im pre CA ti o) — **Ara.**

Improprietas (im pro PRI e tas) — **Acyrologia.**

Inartificial Proofs. Those external to the case and supplied by such things as documents, witnesses, etc. What we would today call "evidence." *See* **Proof.**

Incisum — **Comma.**

Incongruitie. Puttenham's term for **Solecismus.**

Incrementum (in cre MEN tum) — **Auxesis.**

Indignatio (in dig NA ti o; L. "indignation, disdain") — **Aganactesis.** A general term for impassioned speech or loud, angry speaking.

Inductio (in DUC ti o; L. "leading into") — **Epagoge.**

Inductive Proof. Argument, through the various valid forms of syllogism, from an accepted fact or facts to a conclusion based on them; argument from the particular to the general; scientific reasoning.

Informatio (in for MA ti o; L. "representation, sketch, outline")—
Energia.

Insertour. Puttenham's term for **Parenthesis.**

Insultatio (in sul TA ti o) — **Disdainefull.** Derisive, ironical abuse of a person to his face: Dido confronting Aeneas with his desertion of her:

> "Hie thee, and by the wild waves and the wind,
> Seek Italy and Realms for thee to reign,
> If piteous Gods have power amidst the main,
> On ragged rocks thy penance thou mayst find."
>
> (Puttenham)

Intellectio (in tel LEC ti o) — **Synecdoche.**

Intension (L. "stretching, straining"). Generally: connotation of a term; can be more narrowly defined as that part of a term's entire range of meaning which a speaker intends.

Intercusio (in ter CU si o; L. "running between") — **Parenthesis.**

Interjectio (in ter JEC ti o; L. "throwing or placing between, insertion") — **Parenthesis.**

Interpellatio (in ter pel LAH ti o) — **Interruption; Aposiopesis.**

Interpositio (in ter po SIT i o; L. "placing between").

  1. **Parenthesis.**
  2. **Epenthesis.**

Interpretatione (in ter pre ta ti ON e). A repetition or amplification in other words.

Interrogatio (in ter ro GAT i o) — **Erotesis.**

Interruptio (in ter RUP ti o) — **Aposiopesis.**

Interruption. Puttenham's term for **Aposiopesis.**

Inter se Pugnantia (in ter se pug NAN ti a). Pointing out hypocrisy or inconsistency to an opponent's face. Peacham cites Romans 2:21–24:

> "Thou therefore which teachest another, teachest thou
> not thyself? thou that preachest a man should not
> steal, dost thou steal? Thou that sayest a man should
> not commit adultery, dost thou commit adultery?
> thou that abhorrest idols, dost thou commit sacrilege?
> Thou that makest thy boast of the law, through break-
> ing the law dishonourest thou God? For the name of
> God is blasphemed among the Gentiles through you,
> as it is written."

Invention. The first of the five traditional parts of rhetorical theory, concerned with the finding and elaboration of arguments.

L. **Inventio;** G. **Heuresis.**
Inversio (in VER si o) — **Allegory.**
Irmus — Hirmus.
Irony; alt. sp. **Eironeia — Dissimulatio; Enantiosis; Illusio; Drie Mock.** *See also* **Metonymy.**
1. Expressing a meaning directly opposite that intended: "He was no notorious malefactor, but he had been twice on the pillory, and once burnt in the hand for trifling oversights" (Hoskyns).

Generally speaking, the more sophisticated the irony, the more is implied, the less stated.
2. Speaking in derision or mockery:
". . . it was said by a French king, to one that praid his reward, showing how he had been cut in the face at a certain battle fought in his service: ye may see, quoth the king, what it is to run away and look backwards."

(Puttenham)

Specifically rhetorical irony presents few problems. Puttenham's "drie mock" pretty well describes the phenomenon. One kind of rhetorical irony, however, may need further attention. There can be relatively few rhetorical situations where the target of persuasion is utterly ignorant of the designs someone has on him. Even the happiest moron gazing at a TV set must know someone wants him to buy X and not Y. Thus the relationship of persuader and persuaded is almost always self-conscious to some degree. If the persuader wants to overcome any implicit sales-resistance (especially from a sophisticated audience), one of the ways he will do it is to acknowledge that he *is* trying to talk his audience into something. By this, he hopes to gain their trust for as long as the soft sell takes. When he does this, he really acknowledges that his rhetorical maneuvering is ironical, that it says one thing while it tries to do another. At the same time, a second irony is present, since the pitchman is still far from laying all his cards on the table. The point to be made is that every rhetorical posture except the most naïve involves an ironical coloration, of some kind or another, of the speaker's **Ethos.**

From the literary critic's point of view, irony and allegory ought to bear some relation, since irony is clearly a particular, 180-degree-reversed, instance of allegory's double meaning. That is, the ironist depends on an allegorical habit of mind in his reader, a habit that will juxtapose surface and real meanings. The connection of the two terms has not been the subject of any discussion, however. With the recent great interest in the "allegorical temper," on the one hand and the "ironic mode" on the other, perhaps this deficiency may be remedied.

Isocolon (i so COL on; G. "of equal members or clauses") — **Compar; Parison; Parimembre; Even.**

1. Repetition of phrases of equal length and usually corresponding structure.
    a. **Compar:** balancing of two clauses of equal length.
    b. **Parison:** long phrases or clauses in parallel construction sometimes with similar sounds in similar places in the parallel phrases or clauses: Nathaniel to Holofernes:
        "Your reasons at dinner have been sharp
        and sententious; pleasant without scurrility,
        witty without affection, audacious without
        impudency, learned without opinion, and
        strange without heresy."
                (*Love's Labour's Lost*, V, i)
2. G. rhet.: Two or more clauses with the same number of syllables.

Issue — Constitutio; Stasis; Status. Hermagoras, it is generally thought, introduced the theorizing about the *staseis* or issues. The issue was the subject of a debate or the point of contention in a legal action. Hermagoras seems to have distinguished four types:

1. Conjectural (G. *stochasmos*; L. *coniecturalis*): dispute over a fact.
2. Definitional (G. *oros*; L. *definitiva* or *proprietas*): dispute over a definition.
3. Qualitative (G. *cata symbebechlos*; L. *generalis* or *qualitas*): dispute over the value, quality, or nature of an act.
4. Translative (G. *metalepsis*; L. *translativa* or *translatio*): dispute over moving the issue from one court or jurisdiction to another.

Or five: conjectural, definitive, qualitative, quantitative, relative. The *Rhetorica ad Herennium* (I, xi, 18–19) distinguishes three types: conjectural, legal ("some controversy turns upon the letter of a text"), juridical (dispute about fact).

The definition and use of the issues is an extremely vexing problem. One of the fullest discussions is Quintilian's (III, vi; there is also a discussion early in VII), but the Loeb translator warns of it: "This chapter is highly technical and of little interest for the most part to any save professed students of the technique of the ancient schools of rhetoric." There is also a discussion in Howell, *Logic and Rhetoric in England*, pp. 70–71.

Iteratio (i ter A ti o; L. "repetition").
1. **Anaphora.**
2. **Palilogia** (2). Also repetition for fulness.

Iusiurandum (ius iur AN dum) — **Orcos.**

Junctio (JUNC ti o; L. "joining") — **Zeugma.**

Koinoi Topoi (KOI noi   to POI; G. "commonplaces") — **Loci Communes.** *See* 2.3.7.

Koinonia (koi NO ni a; G. "association, partnership"). Consulting with one's opponent or with the judges. *See also* **Comprobatio.**

Koinotes (KOI no tes; G. "sharing in common"; gram. "use of a common word in two clauses") — **Symploce.**

Lamentatio (la men TA ti o; L. "wailing, weeping") — **Threnos.**

Laws of Thought. Those who use this term give three:
1. Principle of Identity — if a statement is true, it is true.
2. Principle of Contradiction — no statement can be both true and false.
3. Principle of Excluded Middle — any statement must be either true or false.

Leptologia (lep to LO gi a; G. "subtlety"). Subtle speaking; quibbling.

Lexis (LEX is; G. "speech; diction, word") — **Elecutio.** *See also* **Style.**

Licentia (li CENT i a; L. "freedom, liberty") — **Parrhesia.**

Licentious. Puttenham's term for **Parrhesia.**

Like Letter. Puttenham's term for **Parimion.**

Like Loose. Puttenham's term for **Homoioteleuton.**

Literal Level. *See* **Allegory.**

Litotes (LIT o tes; G. "plainness, simplicity") — **Diminutio; Exadversio; Moderatour; Tenuitas.** Denial of the contrary; opposite of amplification; understatement that intensifies: "he likes his wife not a little" for "he dotes on her." *See also* **Extenuatio.**

Loci Communes (LO ci   com MUN es) — **Koinoi Topoi.** *See* 2.3.7.

Loci Positio (po SIT i o) — **Topothesia.**

Logic. The rules of formal reasoning. It includes all the devices for persuasion that Aristotle includes under the third group of ways to persuade — "proving the case." The other two are:

1. establishing the speaker as a man of trust;
2. playing on the emotions of the audience.

Long Language. Puttenham's term for **Macrologia.**

Long Loose. Puttenham's term for **Hirmus.**

Loose Language. Puttenham's term for **Asyndeton.**

Loud Lyer. Puttenham's term for **Hyperbole.**

Love Burden. Puttenham's term for **Epimone.**

Macrologia (ma cro LO gi a; G. "speaking at length") — **Perissologia; Pleonasmus; Sermo Superfluus; Long Language.** *See also* **Homiologia.** Long-winded speech; using more words than necessary. Pope quotes Addison:

> "The growth of meadows, and the pride of fields.
> The food of armies and support of wars.
> Refuse of swords, and gleanings of a fight.
> Lessen his numbers, and contract his host.
> Where'er his friends retire, or foes succeed.
> Covered with tempests, and in oceans drowned."
> *(Peri Bathous)*

Mala Affectio (MA la   af FEC ti o; L. "unfavorable impression, attitude, propensity") — **Cacozelia.**

Malapropism. A form of **Cacozelia;** vulgar error through an attempt to seem learned; not, properly speaking, a rhetorical term. The word comes from Mrs. Malaprop, a character in Sheridan's *The Rivals* (1775). Also sometimes **Acyrologia.**

> "MRS. MALAPROP: Now don't attempt to extirpate yourself from the matter: you know I have proof controvertible of it."

Male Collocatum (MAL e   col lo CA tum; L. "badly grouped") — **Cacosyntheton.**

Male Figuratim (fig ur A tim) — **Aschematiston.**

Marching Figure. Puttenham's term for **Climax.**

Martyria (mar TYR i a; G. "testimony, evidence") — **Testatio.** Confirming something by one's own experience, as when Horatio says of the ghost:

> "Before my God, I might not this believe
> Without the sensible and true avouch
> Of mine own eyes."
> *(Hamlet,* I, i)

See also **Apodixis.**

Maxim (L. "greatest [proposition]") — **Proverb.** *See* **Paroemia.** Short pithy statement of a general truth. *See also* **Gnome;**

Sententia; Aphorismus; Adage.

Medela (me DEL a; L. "medicine or cure"). Apology for the undeniable offenses of a friend.

Mediate Inference. One drawn in a syllogism that has two premises; inference from one premise is called *immediate*.

Megaloprepeia (meg a lo pre PEI a; G. "magnificence"). Magnificent, elevated utterance.

Meiosis (mei o sis; G. "lessening") — **Imminutio; Disabler.** To belittle, often through a trope of one word; use a degrading epithet: "childish carriage" for "Rolls Royce." Sometimes is the same as **Litotes,** *q.v.* Quintilian tells us it can also refer to a naturally meager style, or one intentionally and aggressively plain; in the first case it is not a figure, in the second, it is.

Member — Colon.

Membrum Orationis (MEM brum o rat i o nis) — **Colon.**

Memoria (me MOR i a). The Latin term for **Memory.** The Greek is **Mneme.**

Memory — L. **Memoria;** G. **Mneme.** The fourth of the traditional five parts of rhetoric, that which discusses devices to aid and improve the memory.

Mempsis (MEMP sis; G. "blaming, reproach, complaint") — **Querimonia.** Complaining against injuries or pleading for help.

> "How long wilt thou forget me, O Lord? For ever? how long wilt thou hide thy face from me? How long shall I take counsel in my soul, having sorrow in my heart daily? how long shall mine enemy be exalted over me? Consider and hear me, O Lord my God: lighten mine eyes, lest I sleep the sleep of death."
>
> (Psalm 13:1–3)

Merismus (me RIS mus) — **Distribution.**

Merry Scoffe. Puttenham's term for **Asteismus.**

Metabasis (me TAB a sis; G. "change, shifting, transition"); alt. sp. **Medabasis — Transitio.** Figure of transition: brief statement of what has been said and what will follow; a "linking summary" (Taylor).

> "I have hitherto made mention of his noble enterprises in France, and now I will rehearse his worthy acts done near to Rome."
>
> (Peacham)

Metalepsis (me tal EP sis; G. "substitution") — **Transumptio; Far-Fet.** Present effect attributed to a remote cause: "The ship is sinking: damn the wood where the mast grew." The remote cause, because several causal steps intervene between it and the result, seems less like a cause than a metaphor substituted for a cause. Smith (*Mysterie of Rhetorique*) gives the following aberrant definition: "when divers Tropes are shut up in one word: as, 2 *Kings*, 2.9. I pray thee let me have a double portion of thy spirit."

Quintilian (VIII, vi, 37 ff.) calls it a transition from one trope to another. "The commonest example is the following: *cano* is a synonym for *canto* and *canto* for *dico*, therefore *cano* is a synonym for *dico*, the intermediate step being provided by *canto*." The main element would thus seem to be omission of a central term in an extended metaphor.

Metanoia (met a NOI a; G. "repentance; afterthought"); alt. sp. **Metania — Penitent.** *See also* **Correctio.** Qualification of a statement by recalling it and expressing it in a better way, often by using a negative: "He was a prince among men, nay among princes."

Metaphor (G. "transference") — **Translatio; Transport.** *See also* **Metonymy.** Changing a word from its literal meaning to one not properly applicable but analogous to it; assertion of identity rather than, as with **Simile,** likeness. (Quintilian, however, minimizes the differences between the two: "On the whole *metaphor* is a shorter form of *simile*," VIII, vi, 8). Although Aristotle praised metaphor as a primary tool for poetry, the term has never had in rhetoric the protean significance it has taken on in literary criticism. Aristotle's explanation of how a metaphor works has perhaps never been bettered: "midway between the unintelligible and the commonplace, it is a metaphor which most produces knowledge" (*Rhetoric*, III, 1410b). Quintilian calls it "the most beautiful of tropes," praising it for accomplishing "the supremely difficult task of providing a name for everything" (VIII, vi, 4–5).

Metaplasm (MET a plasm; G. "to mold into a new form"). Moving from their natural place the letters or syllables of a word. Generic term. *See* **Prothesis; Aphaeresis; Epenthesis; Syncope; Paragoge; Apocope; Systole; Diastole; Ellipsis; Synaloepha; Synaeresis; Diaeresis;Antisthecon; Metathesis.**

Metastasis (me TAS ta sis; G. "removal, change") — **Remove; Flitting Figure; Transmotio.**

1. Passing over an issue quickly. The cleverest, self-confessed,

example must be Churchill's reply to reporters at a news conference: "I think 'No comment' is a splendid expression. I am using it again and again. I got it from Sumner Welles."

2. Turning back an insult or objection against the person who made it, as when Adam answers Oliver's "Get you with him, you old dog!" with "Is 'old dog' my reward? Most true, I have lost my teeth in your service" (*As You Like It*, I, i).

Metathesis (me TATH e sis; G. "transposition, change") — **Transposition; Antisthecon.** Type of **Metaplasm:** transposition of a letter out of normal order in a word: "morden" for "modern."

Methalemsis (meth a LEM sis) — **Climax.**

Metonymy (me TON y my; G. "change of name") — **Denominatio; Transnominatio; Transmutation; Misnamer.** There are four types corresponding to the four **Causes,** *q.v.* Substitution of cause for effect or effect for cause, proper name for one of its qualities or vice versa; so the Wife of Bath is spoken of as half Venus and half Mars to denote her unique mixture of love and strife. Kenneth Burke (in Appendix D to *A Grammar of Motives*) includes metonymy in his list of four "master tropes." Each, he points out, can perform a function considerably wider than its formal rhetorical definition might indicate:

"For *metaphor* we could substitute *perspective*;

For *metonymy* we could substitute *reduction*;

For *synecdoche* we could substitute *representation*;

For *irony* we could substitute *dialectic*."

Mezozeugma (me zo ZEUG ma) — **Middlemarcher.** Placing in the middle of a construction the common verb on which two or more words or clauses depend: either the full price refund or nothing at all. *See also* **Zeugma.**

Middlemarcher. Puttenham's term for **Mezozeugma.**

Mimesis (mi ME sis; G. "imitation"). Imitation of word or gesture. *See also* **Ethopocia; Characterismus.**

Mingle Mangle. Puttenham's term for **Soriasmus.**

Misnamer. Puttenham's term for **Metonymy.**

Misplacer. Puttenham's term for **Cacosyntheton.**

Mneme (MNE me) — **Memory.**

Moderatour. Puttenham's term for **Litotes.**

Moral Level. *See* **Allegory.**

Multiclinatum (mul ti cli NA tum; L. "leaning toward many") — **Polyptoton.**

Mycterismus (myc ter IS mus; G. "to turn up the nose, sneer at") — **Subsannatio; Fleering Frumpe.** Mockery of an opponent, accompanied by a gesture.

Narration — Praecognitio. The second part of the seven-part classical oration. It tells how the problem at hand had come up, gives the audience, as it were, the history of the problem.

Necessary Cause. A cause in the absence of which the result *cannot* happen.

Necessum (ne CESS um; L. "unavoidable, inevitable") — **Anangeon.**

Newnamer. Puttenham's term for **Onomatopoeia.**

Nicknamer. Puttenham's term for **Prosonomasia.**

Noema (no E ma; G. "thought, idea"). Obscure, subtle speech. Puttenham calls this **Close Conceit.** *See also* **Schematismus; Enigma.**

> "in the United States there is more space where nobody is than where anybody is.
>
> This is what makes America what it is."

(Gertrude Stein, *The Geographical History of America*)

Nominatio (no mi NA ti o; L. "naming").
   1. **Antonomasia.**
   2. **Onomatopoeia.**

Nomini (NO mini) — **Synonym.**

Nominis Fictio (NO mi nis   FIC ti o; L. "feigning of a name") — **Onomatopoeia**

Non Sequitur (SEQ ui tur; L. "it does not follow"). A statement that bears no relationship to the context preceding.

Notatio (no TA ti o; L. "marking, noting, describing") — **Ethopoeia; Characterismus.**

Obtestatio (ob tes TA ti o) — **Deesis.**

Obticentia (ob ti CENT i a; L. "pause, sudden break") — **Aposiopesis.**

Occultatio (oc cul TA ti o; L. "insinuation, suggestion, concealment") — **Occupatio.**

Occupatio (oc cu PA ti o) — **Occultatio; Praeteritio; Paralepsis; Parasiopesis.** A speaker emphasizes something by pointedly seeming to pass over it, as in introducing a guest speaker one says, "I will not dwell here on the twenty books and the thirty articles

Professor X has written, nor his forty years as Dean, nor his many illustrious pupils, but only say . . . ."

Oictros (OIC tros; G. "pitiable"). Gaining forgiveness from another by playing on his pity or moving him to tears. (Taylor lists this as "Cictros," possibly a misreading of the black-letter italics in Sherry.)

Ominatio (o min A ti o). Prophecy of evil. *See also* **Paraenesis; Cataplexis.**

Onedismus (o ne DIS mus; G. "reproach").
  1. **Exprobatio.** reproaching someone as ungrateful or impious.
  2. Any report or character of someone, but usually a bad one.

Onomaton (o NO ma ton; G. "word; noun") — **Scesis Onomaton.**

Onomatopoeia (on o mat o poe I a; G. "the making of words") — **Nominatio; Procreatio; Nominis Fictio; Newnamer.** Use or invention of words that sound like their meaning: "the murmur of innumerable bees"; "riff-raff."

Oppositio (op po SI ti o) — **Antithesis.**

Optatio (op TA ti o). A wish exclaimed: "A horse! my kingdom for a horse."

Oraculum (o RA cu lum; L. "oracle, prophecy"). The quoting of God's Words or Commandments.

Oratory. Public Speech; **Rhetoric,** on the other hand, usually means the *theory* of oratory. There are three types of oratory, corresponding to the three branches of rhetoric:
  1. Deliberative.
  2. Judicial or Forensic.
  3. Epideictic.

Orcos (OR cos; G. "oath") — **Iusiurandum.** An oath.

Ordinatio (or di NA ti o; L. "setting in order, regulating") — **Eutrepismus.**

Ordo Artificialis (OR do ar ti fic i AL is). *See* **Ordo Naturalis.**

Ordo Naturalis (OR do na tur AL is). The term for the "ab ovo" opening of a narrative, common from the *Rhetorica ad Herennium* onward. The opposite term, for the "in medias res" opening, was **Ordo Artificialis.**

Ornatus Difficilis (or NA tus dif FIC i lis) — **Difficult Ornament.**

Outcrie. Puttenham's term for **Ecphonesis.**

Over Labour. Puttenham's term for **Periergia.**

Overreacher. Puttenham's term for **Hyperbole.**

Oxymoron (ox y MOR on; G. "a witty, paradoxical saying"; lit.

"pointedly foolish") — **Synaeceosis.** A condensed paradox, Milton's "darkness visible" for example.

Paeanismus (pae an IS mus; G. "singing of the victory hymn"). An exclamation of joy; a type of **Ecphonesis:**

> "And Mary said, My soul doth magnify the Lord
> And my spirit hath rejoiced in God my Saviour.
> For he hath regarded the low estate of his handmaiden:
> for, behold, from henceforth all generations shall
> call me blessed."

> (Luke 1:46–48)

Palilogia (pal i LO gi a; G. "a recapitulation"). *See* **Enumeratio** (2).

1. **Anadiplosis:** repetition of the last word of one line or clause to begin the next.
2. **Iteratio.** Repetition for vehemence.

Parable (G ."a placing beside"); alt. sp. **Parabola — Resemblance Misticall.** Type of **Homoeosis:** teaching a moral by means of an extended metaphor.

Paradiastole (pa ra di AS to le; G. rhet., "a putting together of dissimilar things").

1. **Distinctio.**
2. **Euphemismus** (2).

Paradiegesis (pa ra di e GE sis; G. "incidental narrative").

1. **Narration.** *See also* **Exemplum.**
2. Using an observation or fact as a point of departure for a further, related observation:

> "Then Paul stood in the midst of Mars' hill, and
> said, Ye men of Athens, I perceive that in all
> things ye are too superstitious. For as I passed
> by, and beheld your devotions, I found an altar
> with this inscription, TO THE UNKNOWN GOD.
> Whom therefore ye ignorantly worship him de-
> clare I unto you. God that made the world and
> all things therein, seeing that he is Lord of heaven
> and earth, dwelleth not in temples made with
> hands; Neither is worshipped with men's hands
> as though he needed any thing, seeing he giveth to
> all life, and breath, and all things."

> (Acts 17:22–25)

Paradigma (pa ra DIG ma; G. "model, example, lesson") — **Exemplum.**

Paradox (G. "contrary to opinion or expectation") — **Wondrer.**
A seemingly self-contradictory statement, which yet is shown to
be (sometimes in a surprising way) true: "She makes the black
night bright by smiling on it."
Paraenesis (pa RAE ne sis; G. "exhortation, recommenda-
tion") — **Admonitio.** Warning of impending evil. *See also*: **Omi-
natio; Cataplexis.**
Paragoge (PARA go ge; G. "leading past") — **Proparalepsis.**
Adding a letter or syllable to the end of a word: "Beforne" for
"Before." *See* **Metaplasm.**
Paralepsis (pa ra LEP sis; G. "disregard, omission"); alt. sp.
Paralipsis — Occupatio; Passager.
Paralogia (pa ra LO gi a; G. "fraudulent reasoning") — **Para-
mologia.**
Paramologia (pa ra mo LO gi a) — **Admittance; Paralogia.** Con-
ceding a point either from conviction of its truth or to use it to
strengthen one's own argument; giving away a weaker point in
order to take a stronger:

> "I deny not but I have heretofore used you in causes
> secret, in matters weighty and of counsel, that I have
> found you friendly, faithfull and ready, but what is
> all that to the purpose, when in a thing so important,
> and matter nearly concerning me, as whereon depend-
> eth the safeguard of my whole house and family, I
> have found you in both negligent and untrusty."
>
> (Day)

Paramythia (pa ra MYTH ı a; G. "encouragement, consola
tion") — **Consolatio.** Consoling one who grieves; a stylized letter or essay of condolence.
Parasiopesis (pa ras i o PE sis; G. "omission, passing over in
silence") — **Occupatio.**
Parataxis (pa ra TAX is; G. "placing side by side"). Clauses or
phrases arranged independently (a coordinate, rather than a sub-
ordinate, construction), sometimes, as here, without the cus-
tomary connectives: "I came, I saw, I conquered." Opposite of
Hypotaxis.
Parathesis (pa ra THE sis; G. "putting beside") — **Parenthesis.**
Parauxesis (par aux E sis) — **Amplificatio.**
Parecbasis (par EC ba sis; G. "deviation, digression"); alt. sp.
Parecnasis — Digression.
Parechesis (par e CHE sis; G. "likeness of sound"). "The repeti-

tion of the same sound in words in close or immediate succession" (Smythe, *Greek Grammar*, p. 680). For example: "Gaunt as the ghastliest of glimpses that gleam through the gloom of the gloaming when ghosts go aghast?" (Swinburne, *Nephelidia*).

Paregmenon (par EG men on; G. "to lead aside, change") — **Polyptoton.**

Parelcon (par EL con; G. "to draw aside or along"). Addition of superfluous words; using two words where only one would normally stand: "for why" instead of "why."

Paremptosis (par emp TO sis) — **Parenthesis.**

Parenthesis (G. "to put in beside") — **Parathesis; Interpositio; Interjectio; Paremptosis; Intercusio; Insertour.** Form of **Hyperbaton:** a word, phrase, or sentence inserted as an aside in a sentence complete in itself.

Pareuresis (par EURE e sis; G. "pretext") — **Adinventio; Excusatio; Excogitata.**

1. Offering an excuse of such weight that it overcomes all objections.

> "By being so long in the lowest form [at Harrow] I gained an immense advantage over the cleverer boys . . . . I got into my bones the essential structure of the ordinary British sentence — which is a noble thing."
>
> (Churchill, *My Early Life*)

2. Inventing a false pretext.

> "FALSTAFF: What, upon compulsion? 'Zounds, an I were at the strappado, or all the racks in the world, I would not tell you on compulsion. Give you a reason on compulsion! if reasons were as plentiful as blackberries, I would give no man a reason upon compulsion, I."
>
> (*I Henry IV*, II, iv)

Parimembre (pari MEM bre) — **Isocolon.**

Parimia — **Paroemia.**

Parimion (par I mi on) — **Like Letter.**

1. A resolute **Alliteration,** in which every word in a phrase or sentence begins with the same letter:

> "HOLOFERNES: The preyful princess pierc'd and prick'd a pretty pleasing pricket."
>
> (*Love's Labour's Lost*, IV, ii)

2. **Alliteration.**

Parison (PAR i son; G. "almost equal"); alt. sp. **Parisosis —
Isocolon.**

Paroemia (pa ROEM i a; G. "byword, proverb"); alt. sp. **Parimia.**
1. **Adage; Proverb; Apothegm; Sententia; Maxim; Aphorismus; Gnome.**
2. Quoting proverbs: as a further source of confusion, the terms in the first definition are sometimes used to mean *quoting* proverbs as well as the proverbs themselves.

Paroemion (pa ROEM i on; G. "closely resembling"); alt. sp.
Paromoeon — Alliteration.

Paromoiosis (par o moi o sis; G. "assimilation, assonance, comparison"); alt. sp. **Paromoeosis.** "Parallelism of sound between the words of two clauses either approximately or exactly equal in size. This similarity in sound may appear at the beginning, at the end (*Homoioteleuton*), in the interior, or it may pervade the whole" (Smythe, *Greek Grammar*, p. 681).

> "Do not let us speak of darker days; let us speak rather
> of sterner days. These are not dark days: these are
> great days."
>
> (Churchill, "To the Boys of Harrow School")

Paronomasia (par on o MAS i a) — **Agnominatio,** *q.v.*; **Adfictio;
Skesis.** Punning; playing on the sounds and meanings of words, unlike **Antanaclasis** in that the words punned on are similar but not identical in sound: Falstaff includes both kinds in jesting with Prince Hal: "Were it not here apparent that thou art heir apparent . . ." (*I Henry IV*, I, ii).
Cicero (*De Oratore*, II, lxiii, 256) gives **Assonance** as a synonym for paronomasia, but although both assonance and **Consonance,** as well as **Alliteration,** might be thought of as kinds of paronomasia, the synonymity has not been accepted.

Parrhesia (parr HES i a; G. "free-spokeness, frankness"); alt. sp.
Parrosia — Licentia; Licentious.
1. Candid speech; Fraunce cites Sidney:
> "I therefore say to thee, O just Judge, that I, and
> only I, was the worker of *Basilius'* death: they
> were these hands that gave unto him that poison-
> ous potion, that has brought death to him, and
> loss to *Arcadia*."
2. **Correctio** (2). Begging pardon in advance for necessary candor.

Partitio (par TIT i o; L. "division; logical division into parts") — **Diaeresis; Proposition.**

Passager. Puttenham's term for **Paralepsis.** *See also* **Occupatio.**

Pathopoeia (path o poe I a; G. "excitement of the passions"); alt. sp. **Pathopopeia** — **Pathos,** *q.v.* General term for arousing passion or emotion. *See also* **Ecphonesis; Deeisis; Optatio; Donysis; Imprecatio;** inter alia.

Pathos (PATH os; G. "to experience, suffer"). This term has been used both for techniques of stirring emotion (especially in a law court) and for the emotions themselves. Further, both the emotions a speaker feels *himself* and those he seeks to evoke in others have some claim to the term. As an additional complication, some writers maintain that the term applies to only certain, or a certain range of, emotions. Thus, Quintilian tells us (VI, ii, 1 ff.) "the more cautious writers" distinguish between pathos, which describes the more violent emotions, and **Ethos,** which refers to the calmer ones. The more violent emotions, too, are likely to be transitory, the calmer ones continuous. It would seem a reasonably correct simplification to say that ethos is the character, or set of emotions, which a speaker reenacts in order to affect an audience. Pathos is the emotion that the speaker aims to induce in his audience, either by his ethos or in any other way. The Renaissance theorists, however, did not make precisely this distinction. Pathos (or pathopoeia) was likely to refer to any emotional appeal, ethos (ethopoeia) simply to a description of character, or of characteristics, for whatever purpose and of whatever kind. The term **Bathos** is sometimes used to describe the emotional appeal that, intentionally or not, evokes laughter rather than transport, which sinks rather than soars.

Penitent. Puttenham's term for **Metanoia.**

Percontatio (per con TA ti o; L. "questioning, inquiry") — **Epiplexis.**

Percursio (per CURS i o) — **Epitrochasmus.**

Periergia (per i ER gi a; G. "overelaboration") — **Macrology; Bomphilogia; Periphrasis; Sedulitas Superflua; Over Labour.** Quintilian makes a case for periergia as, specifically, superfluous elaboration of a point.

Period — **Ambitus; Continuatio; Conclusio; Periodic Sentence.** *See also* **Clausula.** The third and longest element in the classical theory of the Period, an (originally Peripatetic) theory of prose rhythm. Quintilian (IX, iv, 19 ff.) distinguishes two styles:

"There are then in the first place two kinds of style: the one is closely welded and woven together, while the other is of a looser texture such as is found in dialogues and letters." The first or "compact," is for him the one to which the **Comma-Colon-Period** theory of prose rhythm properly applies. Others apply it especially to formal oratorical or declamatory occasions. The basic unit of measurement is the period. If this grows too long, however, some see the colon or **Member** as the basic unit (see Croll, *Style, Rhetoric, and Rhythm,* pp. 324 ff.). Its parts are cola; the components of the cola are short often parenthetical elements, the commata. The exact nature of these divisions is very variously defined and defies simplification. (They are not to be confused with the punctuation marks that later took over their names, of course.) Perhaps the following suggestions will help.

1. The period for Aristotle (*Rhetoric,* III, 1409ª ff.): "By a period I mean a portion of speech that has in itself a beginning and an end, being at the same time not too big to be taken in at a glance . . . . The period must . . . not be completed until the sense is complete.

   "A Period may be either divided into several members or simple. The period of several members is a portion of speech (1) complete in itself, (2) divided into parts, and (3) easily delivered at a single breath . . . . A member is one of the two parts of such a period. By a 'simple' period, I mean that which has only one member. The members, and the whole period, should be neither curt nor long.

   "The periodic style which is divided into members is of two kinds. It is either simply divided . . . or it is antithetical."

2. Demetrius' *On Style* distinguishes three types of period, corresponding roughly to the traditional levels of style:
   a. Historical (low) — plain, simple, suited to description.
   b. Conversational (middle) — loosest, least periodic.
   c. Rhetorical (high) — ornamental, highly periodic.

3. Generally speaking one might say that the period expresses a complete thought self-sufficiently; beyond this, it must have at least two members. (Cicero insists it must not be longer than four iambic trimeters.) "Periodic Sentence" is a very rough English equivalent; it describes a long sentence that consists of a number of elements, often balanced or antithetical, and existing in perfectly clear syntactical

relationship to one another. The phrase "suspended syntax" is often used 'to describe it, since the syntactical pattern, and so the sense, is not completed, is "suspended" until the end. The effect of the periodic sentence is often to throw the interest forward, create a mild suspense. So Dr. Johnson on Shakespeare's annotators: "I could have written longer notes, for the art of writing notes is not of difficult attainment. The work is performed, first by railing at the stupidity, negligence, ignorance, and asinine tastelessness of the former editors, and showing, from all that goes before and all that follows, the inelegance and absurdity of the old reading; then by proposing something which to superficial readers would seem specious, but which the editor rejects with indignation; then by producing the true reading, with a long paraphrase, and concluding with loud declamations on the discovery and a sober wish for the advancement and prosperity of genuine criticism." The climactic member need not be at the end, however. Sometimes it is at the center, whence the terms "circuitus" and "round composition."

Periodic Sentence — Period (1).

Periphrasis (pe RIPH ra sis; G. "circumlocution") — **Circuitio; Ambage.** Circumlocution.

Perissologia (per iss o LO gi a; G. "wordiness; elaborate writing") — **Macrologia.**

Peristasis (per IST a sis; G. "circumstances, situation"). Amplifying by describing attendant circumstances.

Peristrophe (per IST ro phe; G. "a turning around"). Converting an opponent's argument to one's own use. So a peculating tax-collector might say: "Yes, I took bribes; on my salary I had to."

Permissio (per MISS i o) — **Concessio.**

Permutatio (per mu TA ti o; L. "change, substitution").
1. **Enullage.**
2. **Antimetabole.**

Peroration — Conclusion; Epilogue. The last part of the seven-part classical oration. This conclusion was often an *impassioned* summary, not simply a review of previous arguments.

Perseverentia (per se ver EN ti a; L. "constancy; long — and so tedious — continuance") — **Epimone.**

Personification — Prosopopoeia. An animal or an inanimate object is represented as having human attributes or addressed as if it were human:

> "So saying, her rash hand in evil hour
> Forth reaching to the Fruit, she pluck'd, she eat:
> Earth felt the wound, and Nature from her seat
> Sighing through all her Works gave signs of woe,
> That all was lost."
>
> (Milton, *Paradise Lost*, XI, 780 ff.)

Persuasion. The goal of **Rhetoric.** Aristotle lists three modes:
1. The character of the orator.
2. Putting the audience in the right mood.
3. Proving, or seeming to prove, the case.

Perversio (per VER si o; L. "inversion") — **Anastrophe.**

Petitio Principii (pe TIT i o   prin CIP i i; L. "begging the question"). The premise and conclusion say the same thing in different words, or the premise needs proof as much as the conclusion. One might argue, for example, that poverty is a good thing since the right to starve is a Basic American Freedom. *See* **Fallacy (Logical).**

Philophronesis (PHI lo phron E sis; G. "kind treatment") — **Benevolentia.** Attempt to mitigate anger by gentle speech and humble submission:

> "And Jacob sent messengers before him to Esau his
> brother unto the land of Seir, the country of Edom.
> And he commanded them, saying, Thus shall ye
> speak unto my lord Esau; Thy servant Jacob saith
> thus, I have sojourned with Laban, and stayed there
> until now: And I have oxen, and asses, flocks, and
> menservants, and womenservants: and I have sent
> to tell my lord, that I may find grace in thy sight."
>
> (Gen. 32:3–5)

Phrasis (PHRA sis; G. "way of speaking"). The term is sometimes used to mean "diction," or "idiom," sometimes to mean **Style.**

Pleonasmus (ple on AS mus; G. "excess") — **Macrologia; Too Full Speech.** Needless repetition: "I spoke the words with my own mouth."

Ploce (PLO ce; G. "plaiting") — **Traductio; Copulatio; Conexio; Diaphora; Swift Repeate.** Repetition of a word with a new signification after the intervention of another word or words.

Peacham would confine this term to repetition of a proper name, specifying diaphora for repetition of ordinary words:

> "He whilest he liued, happie was through thee,
> And being dead is happie now much more;
> Liuing, that lincked chaunst with thee to bee,
> And dead, because him dead thou dost adore
> As liuing, and thy lost deare loue deplore."

(Spenser, *The Rvines of Time*)

See also **Epanodos** (2); **Epiploce.**

Poiciologia (poi ci o LO gi a; G. "intricate wording"). Awkward, ungrammatical speech.

Pointed Style. This phrase is used in discussions of seventeenth-century prose style to refer to a style usually **Senecan,** *q.v.*, in which rhetorical figures (often schemes, especially those of balance and antithesis, of word- and sound-play) are used to clarify, reinforce, "point" a meaning. The effect is often epigrammatic. The pointed style, neat and concise, witty, can thus be contrasted with a witty style ornamented for the sake of ornament itsclf, rather than for an enhancement of meaning. The noun "point" often meant the **Sententia,** or meaning, which was thus epigrammatically expressed. Seneca is usually quoted as the exemplar of the pointed style; in English, Lincoln offers a familiar example: "It is true that you may fool all the people some of the time; you can even fool some of the people all of the time; but you cannot fool all of the people all of the time." (For a fuller discussion of pointed style, see Williamson, *The Senecan Amble*, chap. 3.)

Polyptoton (po lyp TO ton; G. "employment of the same word in various cases"); alt. sp. **Polyptiton — Paregmenon; Adnominatio; Traductio** (2); **Multiclinatum.** Repetition of words from the same root but with different endings: "Society is no comfort to one not sociable."

Polysyndeton (poly SYN de ton) — **Coople Clause.** Use of a conjunction between each clause; opposite of **Asyndeton.** Milton says of Satan, in his course through Chaos, that he

> "pursues his way,
> And swims, or sinks, or wades, or creeps, or flies."

(*Paradise Lost*, II, 949–950)

Pompous Speech. Puttenham's term for **Bomphiologia.**

Post Hoc Ergo Propter Hoc (L. "after this, therefore because of this"). Assigning the wrong cause, mistaking a temporal for a causal relationship.

Praecedens Correctio (prae CE dens   cor REC ti o) — **Correctio** (2).

Praeceptio (prae CEP ti o; L. "taking beforehand") — **Procatalepsis.**

Praecisio (prae CIS i o) — **Aposiopesis.**

Praecognitio (prae cog NIT i o; L. "foreknowledge") — **Narration.**

Praeexercitamina (prae ex er ci TA min a; L. "preparatory exercises") — **Progymnasmata.**

Praegnans Constructio (PRAEG nans   con STRUC ti o; L. "swollen construction") — **Ellipsis.** A type of **Brachylogia,** *q.v.*, where two phrases or clauses are condensed into one: "He will directly to the lords."

Praemunitio (prae mu NIT i o; L. "strengthening beforehand"); alt. sp. **Premunitio.**

   1. **Proposition** (1).

   2. **Procatasceue.**

Praeoccupatio (prae oc cu PA ti o) — **Procatalepsis.**

Praeparatio (prae par A ti o) — **Procatasceue.**

Praesumptio (prae SUMP ti o) — **Procatalepsis.**

Praeteritio (prae ter IT i o; L. "a passing over") — **Occupatio.**

Pragmatographia (prag ma to GRAPH i a; G. "description of an action, affair") — **Counterfalt Action.** Type of Hypotyposis: vivid description of an action or event.

Precatio (pre CA ti o; L. "prayer") — **Euche.**

Prepostera Locutio — **Hysterologia** (2).

Preposterous. Puttenham's term for **Hysteron Proteron.**

Presumptuous. Puttenham's term for **Procatalepsis.**

Principle of Contradiction. One of the three "laws of thought." It states: No statement can be both false and true.

Principle of Excluded Middle. One of the three "laws of thought." It states: Any statement must be either true or false.

Principle of Identity. One of the three "laws of thought." It states: If a statement is true, it is true.

Privie Nippe. Puttenham's term for **Charientismus.**

Procatalepsis (pro ca tal EP sis; G. "anticipation") — **Praeoccupatio; Praeceptio; Praesumptio; Presumptuous; Ante Occupatio; Anticipatio; Prolepsis** (2). Anticipating an objection and preventing it:

"But some man will say, How are the dead raised up? and with what body do they come? Thou fool, that which thou sowest is not quickened, except it die: And that which thou sowest, thou sowest not that body shall be, but bare grain, it may chance wheat, or of some other grain."

(I Corinthians 15:35–37)

Procatasceue (pro cat a SCEU e; G. "prepare beforehand"); alt. sp. **Proparascene** — **Praemunitio** (2); **Praeparatio.** Giving an audience a gradual preparation and buildup before telling them about something done. *See also* **Correctio** (2); **Procatalepsis.**

Proclees (PRO clees; G. "challenge") — **Provocatio.** Vehement challenge to action.

Procreatio (pro cre A ti o) — **Onomatopoeia.**

Prodiorthosis (pro di or THO sis; G. "setting right by anticipation") — **Correctio** (2).

Proecthesis (pro EC the sis; G. "introduction, prefatory account").

1. Peacham uses it to mean defending what one has done or said, by giving reasons and circumstances. His example (Mark 3:2–6) does not seem really to the point, however, especially in view of Quintilian's definition, which follows.
2. Quintilian's definition differs slightly from the above: "pointing out what ought to have been done, and then what actually has been done."
3. *Rhetorica ad Herennium* (IV, xxiv, 34) makes proecthesis really a branch of **Hypophora,** *q.v.*

Progressio (pro GRESS i o).

1. Advancing by steps of comparison to the most important point of a series:
   "What a boy art thou in comparison of this fellow here. Thou sleeps: he wakes: thou plays: he studies: thou art ever abroad: he is ever at home: thou never waits, he still doth his attendance: thou carest not for no body: he doeth his duty to all men: thou doest what thou canst to hurt all, and please none: he doeth what he can to hurt none, and please all."

   (Wilson)
2. **Auxesis.**

Progymnasmata (pro gym NAS ma ta; G. "prefatory exercises").

The title of (and hence generic name for) the Greek rhetorician Hermogenes' list of rhetorical exercises. Examples: fable, narrative, amplification, maxim, refutation, confirmation, etc. Priscian translated them as **Praeexercitamina.**

Prolepsis (pro LEP sis; G. "preconception, anticipation") — **Propounder.**

1. Applying now an attribute or epithet that will have relevancy later: "You're wounded! Nay . . . I'm killed, Sire!"
2. **Procatalepsis.**
3. **Epanados.**

Pronominatio (pro no mi NA ti o) — **Antonomasia.**

Prooemium (pro OEM i um; G. "opening") — **Exordium.**

Proof. Aristotle's *Rhetoric* isolates three areas or types of proof available to an orator:

1. *Ethos,* or the demonstration of the speaker's good character;
2. *Pathos,* or playing on the audience's feelings;
3. *Logos,* logical proof (subdivided into *enthymeme* and *example*).

The first two had formerly been part of the peroration rather than the argument, properly so called. He thus planted the seed of the Ramist controversy of the sixteenth century, where a group of theorists wished once again to separate the first two categories from the third.

Care should be exercised not to equate "proof" and "scientific proof." There were three types of reasoning for Aristotle (scientific demonstration, dialectic, rhetoric), and each had its own "proof." Rhetoric, for example, used the enthymeme, or probable syllogism, where scientific demonstration used the syllogism, properly so called because its conclusions were universally, not generally, true. *See also* 2.3.5.

Proparalepsis (pro para LEP sis).

1. **Paragoge.** Adding a syllable to the end of a word; "dampen" for "damp."
2. Adding a syllable to a word.

Proportio (pro POR ti o; L. "proportion, symmetry, analogy") — **Analogy.**

Proposition — Partitio.

1. Rhet.: The fourth part of the seven-part classical oration.

It briefly stated the proposition to be proved, or the problem to be solved.
2. Log.: A statement in which something is affirmed or denied. There are two kinds:
   a. Primary — about things; "This is a chair."
   b. Secondary — about other propositions; "I think this is a chair."

Propounder. Puttenham's term for **Prolepsis.**

Prosapodosis (pros a PO do sis) — **Prosopoesis; Redditio.** Supporting each alternative with a reason; a distributive reply: "He must either love her or leave her: love her, to stay together; leave her, to gain peace of mind."
See also **Apophasis.**

Prosonomasia (pros on o MA si a; G. "naming, appellation") — **Nicknamer.**
1. Calling by a name or nickname:
   "As, *Tiberius* the Emperor, because he was a
   great drinker of wine, they called him by way of
   derision to his own name, *Caldius Biberius Mero,*
   instead of *Claudius Tiberius Nero.*"
                                            (Puttenham)
2. Confused by some rhetoricians (following Day) with **Paronomasia.**

Prosopoesis (pros o POE sis) — **Prosapodosis.**

Prosopographia (pros o po GRAPH i a; G. "face, countenance, person") — **Counterfait Countenance.**
1. A type of **Hypotyposis:** Description of imaginary persons or bodies such as have never really existed.
2. Lively description of a person. *See also* **Topographia; Chorographia; Chronographia; Geographia; Hydrographia; Anemographia; Dendrographia:**
   "It was to weet a wilde and saluage man,
       Yet was no man, but onely like in shape,
       And eke in stature higher by a span,
       All ouergrowne with haire, that could awhape
       An hardy hart, and his wide mouth did gape
       With huge great tecth, like to a tusked Bore:
       For he liu'd all on rauin and on rape
       Of men and beasts; and fed on fleshly gore,
   The signe whereof yet stain'd his bloudy lips afore."
                            (Spenser, *Faerie Queene,* IV, vii, 5)

Prosopopoeia (pro so po poe ɪ a) — **Conformatio; Personification; Counterfait in Personation.** *See also* **Sermocinatio.**
  1. An imaginary or absent person is represented as speaking or acting:
    "And *Mole* himselfe, to honour her the more,
      Did deck himself in freshest faire attire,
      And his high head, that seemeth alwaies hore
      With harned frosts of former winters ire,
      He with an Oaken girlond now did tire,
      As if the loue of some new Nymph late seene,
      Had in him kindled youthfull fresh desire,
      And made him change his gray attire to greene;
    Ah gentle *Mole!* such ioyance hath thee well beseen."
            (Spenser, *Faerie Queene*, VII, vii, 11)
  2. **Personification.**
Prosthesis (PROS the sis; G. "placing before or in public"). Adding a letter or syllable to the beginning of a word: "irregardless" for "regardless."
Protrope (PRO tro pe; G. "exhortation") — **Adhortatio.** Exhorting hearers to act by threats or promises:
      "Seeming, seeming!
    I will proclaim thee, Angelo; look for 't:
    Sign me a present pardon for my brother,
    Or with an outstretch'd throat I'll tell the world aloud
    What man thou art."
            (*Measure for Measure*, II, iv)
Proverb (L. "an old saying") — **Gnome; Maxim; Sententia; Aphorismus; Adage.** A short, pithy statement of a general truth, one that condenses into memorable form common experience. Each of the words above is often used as a synonym for one or more of the others. They may carry various weights of authority to certain audiences (a sententia may be more weighty than an aphorism) but no firm distinctions have gained real hold. A distinction between proverbs and adages as the wisdom of a group of men, and apothegms, maxims and sentences, as the wisdom of one man, has been advanced. One scholar has recently distinguished proverb, a common saying that has become fixed (and often alliterative) in form, from a sententia, where the common wisdom has not yet found a fixed and widely accepted form. This would not seem to agree fully with Quintilian's labeling of gnomes as *sententiae* (L. "judgments") because they resemble the for-

malism of decisions by public bodies. Another scholar defines
sentential as a fine saying, proverb as a common saying; here,
too, the distinction is not commonly accepted. The resemblance
of the proverb to the commonplace or *topos* is clear enough.
The proverb is a commonplace at a further remove of generality.
It can be viewed as the last stage of generality for the exemplum.
The most difficult thing for the modern reader to remember is
that the proverb, like the **Exemplum,** has been for most of formal
rhetoric's history a means of *proof* rather than a substantiating
ornament. A second lesson for the modern reader, annoyed as he
often is by the solemn plethora of proverbial wisdom in the
earlier literature, would seem to be the lesson Polonius teaches.
In imaginative literature (and this is certainly true of imaginative
literature of the English Renaissance), the proverb is, very likely,
ironical. And, not infrequently, it may be so wide of the point
as to be ludicrously irrelevant, a comic device. The literary use
of proverbs usually is a device to introduce the commonly accepted ideas and attitudes of a society into a situation they cannot deal with. Naturally they will flounder. This common use has
been seen in Polonius' case easily enough (though "to thine own
self be true" still makes the purple patch recitals by famous
actors), but it is commonly ignored elsewhere in the earlier literature. The point here would seem to be that the precise *kind* of
proverb (or the precise term for it) matters less than the way it is
used in a specific text. Perhaps the terms will have readily sepa-
rable meanings only when the use of the proverb in enough different texts has been described to make the many different terms
really necessary to describe the full range of use. *See also* **Paroemia.**

Provocatio (pro VO CA ti o) — **Proclees.**

Prozeugma (pro ZEUG ma; G. "to join in front") — **Ringleader.**
The verb is expressed in the first clause and understood in the
others: "Pride oppresseth humility; hatred love; cruelty compas-
sion" (Peacham).
See also **Zeugma.**

Pseudomenos (pseu DO men os; G. "to lie; be forsworn"). An
argument that puts the adversary in a position where he must tell
a lie, whatever he says: ask a Cretan — proverbial liars —
whether all Cretans are liars.

Pun (etymology uncertain) — **Antanaclasis; Syllepsis; Paronomasia; Asteismus.**

Pysma (PYS ma; G. "question") — **Quaesitio.** Asking many questions that require diverse answers. Imogen to Pisanio, in *Cymbeline*:

> "Why good fellow,
> What shall I do the while? Where bide? how live?
> Or in my life what comfort, when I am
> Dead to my husband?"
>
> (III, iv)

Quadrivium (qua DRIV i um; L. "a place where four roads meet; the four mathematical sciences"). The traditional medieval curriculum leading to the M.A.; it was composed of arithmetic, geometry, astronomy, and music. Together with the **Trivium,** *q.v.*, it comprised the seven liberal arts.

Quaesitio (quae SIT i o; L. "seeking or searching after") — **Pysma.**

Qualifier. Puttenham's term for **Epitheton.**

Quarreller. Puttenham's term for **Antitheton;** *see* **Antithesis.**

Quaternio Terminorum (qua TER ni o   term in OR um). Fallacy of having a categorical syllogism with four or more terms.

Querimonia (quer i MON i a; L. "complaint") — **Mempsis.**

Questioner. Puttenham's term for **Erotesis.**

Quick Conceite. Puttenham's term for **Synecdoche.**

Ratiocinatio (rat i o ci NA ti o; L. "calm reasoning; reasoning by asking questions"). A question addressed by the speaker to himself. *See also* **Erotesis; Apostrophe; Hypophora.**

> "What's this, what's this? Is this her fault or mine?
> The tempter or the tempted, who sins most?"
>
> (*Measure for Measure*, II, ii)

Reason Rend. Puttenham's term for **Aetiologia.**

Rebounde. Puttenham's term for **Antanaclasis.**

Reciprocatio (re cip ro CA ti o; L. "regression, going back on oneself") — **Antanaclasis.**

Recompencer. Puttenham's term for **Antanagoge.**

Recordatio (re cor DA ti o; L. "recalling to mind") — **Anamnesis.**

Redditio (red DI ti o; L. "giving back, rendering a reason") — **Prosapodosis.**

Redditio Causae (CAU sae) — **Aetiologia.**

Redditio Contraria (con TRAR i a) — **Antapodosis.**

Reditus ad Propositum (RED i tus   ad   pro POS i tum). Return to the proposition after a digression.

Redouble. Puttenham's term for **Anadiplosis.**

Reductio ad Absurdum (re DUC ti o ad ab SURD um; L. "reducing to absurdity"). To disprove a proposition one validly deduces from it a conclusion self-contradictory or contradictory to acknowledged fact.

Reduplicatio (re du pli CA ti o) — **Anadiplosis.**

Refractio (re FRAC ti o; L. "breaking open") — **Antanaclasis.**

Refutation — **Confutation; Applicatio.** The sixth part of the seven-part classical oration. This part answered the opponent's objections.

Regressio — **Epanados.**

Reinforcer. Puttenham's term for **Emphasis.**

Rejectio (re JEC ti o) — **Apodioxis.**

Relatio (re LA ti o; L. "bringing back, return") — **Anaphora.**

Remove. Puttenham's term for **Metastasis.**

Repetitio (re pe TIT i o).
1. **Anaphora.**
2. **Epanalepsis.**

Replie. Puttenham's term for **Symploce.**

Report. Puttenham's term for **Anaphora.**

Rerewarder. Puttenham's term for **Hypozeugma.**

Resemblance by Imagerie. Puttenham's term for **Icon.**

Resemblance Misticall. Puttenham's term for **Parable.**

Responce. Puttenham's term for **Anthypophora.**

Restrictio (re STRIC ti o; L. "restriction, limitation"). Excepting part of a statement already made.

> "That it should come to this!
> But two months dead: nay, not so much, not two."
>   (*Hamlet*, I, ii)

Reticentia (re ti CEN ti a) — **Aposiopesis.**

Retire. Puttenham's term for **Epanodos.**

Reversio (re VER si o) — **Anastrophe.**

Rhetoric. Traditionally, the art of rhetoric was invented in the early fifth century B.C. in Sicily, since at that time the overthrow of the Syracusan tyrants had created a great deal of litigation. A later tradition has the famous sophist Gorgias of Leontini bringing it to Athens in 427. (See Quintilian, III, i, 8 ff.) But if we define rhetoric broadly as the "Art of Persuasion," its basic techniques must have been first tried out against Eve, not against the Syracusan tyrants. What Syracuse contributed, if the tradition is true, must have been a body of sophisticated theory.

Rhetoric, as a body of traditional theory (the second of the seven liberal arts) conveniently if too-simply defined as the "Art of Persuasion," has always tended to outgrow its original concern with public speaking, or direct verbal communication, and to lend itself to written communication as well. It has from earliest times vacillated between a concern with specific techniques only, available to the good and bad cause alike, and a larger ethical concern that continually tempts it to say that all persuasion is virtuous persuasion. Cato's definition of an orator as *vir bonus, dicendi peritus* (a good man, skilled in speaking) can stand for this second position as well as any, and would seem to bring almost all humane learning into the domain of rhetoric (as, indeed, seems to happen in *De Oratore*). Most theorists have taken as rhetoric's arena some ground measured between these two extremes. In Bacon's famous definition, for example ("The duty and office of rhetoric is to apply reason to imagination for the better moving of the will") the ethical concern of rhetoric comes in almost as an assumption — "*duty* and office." Quintilian, on the other hand, though he emphasized the moral obligation of the orator, defined the art as one whose "end and highest aim is to speak well."

Cicero held that the orator had three "offices" or main functions: to teach, to please, to move. The area these three cover may indicate why rhetorical theory has so often, in its history, overlapped poetics. To draw the analogy between poetry and rhetoric on the one hand and pure and applied science on the other (poetry: pure science/rhetoric: applied science) may explain something about the domains of the two bodies of theory, but it by no means fully distinguishes them. Another categorization that may sometimes help is the one Kenneth Burke suggests (*Rhetoric of Motives*, pp. 573–574) between persuasion to feel and persuasion to do, between attitude and act. An antislavery poem leads us to commiserate with slaves; an antislavery rhetoric leads us to free them. The difficulties of this distinction as a general one are clear, of course, the most obvious being that since the feeling must precede the act, poetry and rhetoric would become simply two stages or degrees of persuasion. A third criterion of differentiation between the two might be this: rhetoric aims to induce an emotion or state of mind which can be created in other ways as well (there are many ways to drive someone mad), while poetry aims to create an emotion in its audience which is (or aims to be) inseparable from the means used to create it (Lear's madness — and our response to it — are like no others). But this distinction hardly satisfies, either. In the area where the two bodies of theory overlap, the connotative, suggestive, metaphoric use of language, one must have recourse to whatever set of categories suits the present purpose.

As a parallel case of overlapping domains, one might adduce the (originally Platonic) conflict between rhetoric and philosophy. Plato argued (first in the *Gorgias*, then less harshly in the *Phaedrus*) that rhetoric was a sham art, really no art at all, because — concerned only with deception — it could have no true subject matter. Aristotle's counterargument, that rhetoric had to do with the *available means* of persuasion, and was thus as much a practical art as any other, would seem to have settled the question, at least for all those who think that to know the truth is not always to follow it. To rhetoric Plato opposed dialectic, the means of searching out truth. This oversimplified distinction has lingered, so that "mere rhetoric" means artful sometimes fanciful lying. The persuasive form a truth comes dressed in is, in this conception, part of the truth itself. A final separation between rhetoric and philosophy seems as impossible as one between rhetoric and poetry. Kennedy (*The Art of Persuasion in Greece*, p. 15) sums up the problem as well as anyone:

"The disagreement between Plato and the sophists over rhetoric was not simply an historical contingency, but reflects a fundamental cleavage between two irreconcilable ways of viewing the world. There have always been those, especially among philosophers and religious thinkers, who have emphasized goals and absolute standards and have talked much about truth, while there have been as many others to whom these concepts seem shadowy or imaginary and who find the only certain reality in the process of life and the present moment. In general, rhetoricians and orators, with certain distinguished exceptions, have held the latter view, which is the logical, if unconscious, basis of their common view of art as a response to a rhetorical challenge unconstrained by external principles. The difference is not only that between Plato and Gorgias, but between Demosthenes and Isocrates, Virgil and

Ovid, Dante and Petrarch, and perhaps Milton and
Shakespeare."

A third instance of conflicting areas of theory is the relation of
logic (dialectic) to rhetoric. This relationship, in the Greek and
Latin theorists, is extremely complex. The widest generalization
might be that rhetoric was the theory of popular communication,
logic, of learned communication. Thus rhetoric was often compared to the open palm, available to all, logic to the closed fist.
For the student of English rhetorical theory, the main conflict
centered on the teachings of Peter Ramus (Pierre de la Ramée,
1515–1572). Howell (*Logic and Rhetoric in England*, p. 148)
has summarized these, as follows:

> "He ordained that logic should offer training in in-
> vention and arrangement, with no help whatever from
> rhetoric. He ordained that the topic of arrangement
> should take care of all speculations regarding the meth-
> od of discourse, with no help whatever from inven-
> tion. He ordained that rhetoric should offer training
> in style and delivery, and that style should be limited
> to the tropes and the schemes, with no help whatever
> from grammar, which was to be assigned only subject
> matter derived from considerations of etymology and
> syntax. The subject of memory, which we have seen
> to be a recognized part of traditional rhetoric since the
> youth of Cicero, was detached by Ramus from rhetoric,
> and was not made a special topic elsewhere in his
> scheme for the liberal arts, except so far as logic helped
> memory indirectly by providing the theoretical basis
> for strict organization of discourse."

Rhetoric thus becomes, for Ramus, largely a matter of verbal
ornament of style. (This conception of rhetoric as a theory of
verbal ornament is one of the three types of theorizing Howell
finds in England in the Renaissance; the other two are *Ciceronian*,
which adheres to the five-part traditional division of the art of
rhetoric, and *formulary*, which teaches through a collection of
examples. For a fuller discussion, see Howell, chap. 3.)

By an odd quirk which may reveal something of the naïve na-
tional character, "rhetoric," in American education, has come to
be synonymous with "prose composition." The underlying assumption of such a synonymity must be that the student, once he
knows the arts of language, will use them to present clear mean-

ings and present them clearly, rather than to deceive. There is no reason not to use "rhetoric" in this way, but no one should mistake such a hopeful redefinition for the historical one.

Rhetorical Syllogism. One in which the premises are only generally, not absolutely (scientifically proved), true. *See* **Enthymeme** (3).

Rhodian Style. The middle style between **Atticism** and **Asiatismus,** *q.v.*

Right Reasoner. Puttenham's term for **Dialogismus.**

Ringleader. Puttenham's term for **Prozeugma.**

Sage Sayer. Puttenham's term for **Sententia.**

Sarcasmus (sar CAS mus; G. lit. "to tear flesh, gnash teeth") — **Amara Irrisio; Exacerbatio; Bitter Taunt.** A bitter gibe or taunt: "The Pope in this life sells heaven, hell therefore he reserveth to himself in the life to come" (Smith).

Scesis Onomaton (SCE sis o NO ma ton; G. "relation of words").
   1. A sentence constructed of substantives and adjectives only:
        "A maid in conversation chaste, in speech mild,
        in countenance cheerful, in behavior modest, in
        beauty singular, in heart humble and meek, in
        honest mirth, merry with measure. . . ."
                                                                (Peacham)
   2. Using a string of synonymous expressions: "We sinned; we acted unjustly, we perpetrated evil."

Schematismus (sche ma TIS mus; G. "configuration"). Circuitous speech. *See also* **Noema; Enigma.**

Scheme (G. "form, figure").
   1. Any kind of figure or pattern of words.
   2. A figure of arrangement of words in which the literal sense of the word is not affected by the arrangement. *See* **Trope.**

Second Sophistic. The Atticism, in imitation of the early Greek sophists, which became increasingly important in Rome from the second half of the first century, and which tended to obscure both Latin rhetorical theory and practice and the cultivation, especially, of Latin *kunstprosa.*

Secundum Quid (se CUN dum). *A dicto simpliciter ad dictum secundum quid.* Reasoning that because something is generally true, it is true in a highly specialized class: "To imprison a man is cruel; therefore, murderers should be allowed to run free." *See* **Fallacy (Logical).**

Securitas (se CUR i tas; L. "freedom from care") — **Asphalia.**
Sedulitas Superflua (se DUL i tas su PER flu a; L. "excessive zeal") — **Periergia.**
Selfe Saying. Puttenham's term for **Tautologia.**
Senecan Style. The paratactic style of the Latin moralist Lucius Annaeus Seneca, which is usually contrasted with the Ciceronian period. As a term in English studies, Senecan style usually means the anti-Ciceronian prose of the late sixteenth and early seventeenth centuries. The scholar who is still the authority in this field, the late Morris W. Croll, called this style the *Attic*, harking back to the classical distinction between the *Asiatic*, or highly figured, and the *Attic*, or plainer style. Croll's description of this plainer style, as it was manifest in the seventeenth century, has been neatly summarized by Jonas Barish in "Baroque Prose in the Theater: Ben Jonson," *PMLA*, LXIII (June, 1958):

> "The curt style, or, as it was sometimes called, the *stile coupé* or *stile serré*, owes its various names to its abruptness and jaggedness in contrast to Ciceronian "roundness;" and its characteristic device is the so-called "exploded period," composed of independent members set off from each other not by syntactic ligatures but by colons or semicolons (or, in the case of dramatic prose, often by commas). The members of such a period tend to brevity, as the name suggests, but also to irregularity of length, variation in form, and unpredictability of order, a set of traits which, as Croll observes, communicates the effect of live thinking rather than logical premeditation. The "mere fact" or main idea of the period is liable to be exhausted in the first member; subsequent members explore the idea imaginatively, by means of metaphor, aphorism, or example, rather than through ordered analysis."

The seventeenth-century variation, or mutation, of the Ciceronian style (that is, the looser of the anti-Ciceronian styles), Barish summarizes this way:

> "The loose style, Croll's other subcategory of the baroque, differs from the curt style in that it prefers to multiply connectives rather than to suppress them. It tends also to longer members and longer periods, but its character is determined by its habit of heaping up con-

junctions and by the kind of conjunctions it chooses —
simple coordinates such as *and* and *or*, which involve
the least possible syntactic commitment to what has
gone before, and even more typically, the stricter relative and subordinating conjunctions used as though
they were mere coordinates. And all of this is done,
as Croll urges, in order to free the period from formal
restraints, to enable it to move with the utmost license
from point to point, to follow nothing but the involu-
tions of the thinking mind. For the enchaining sus-
pensions of the Ciceronian period, the loose style
substitutes its own devices, the parenthesis and the
absolute construction."

The uses of these two baroque, or, loosely, Senecan styles Barish
then summarizes:

"If the curt style is peculiarly suited to expressions of
quick wit, excitement, distraction, and the like, the
loose style, by virtue of its greater floridity, lends itself well to purposes of formal declamation."

Scholars desiring more information than the scope of this listing
permits should consult the Croll and Williamson volumes listed
in chapter 7, as well as the two Barish articles.

Sentence — Period. Croll pointed out that "sentence" was a grammatical, "period" a rhetorical, term, but this distinction has not
been generally maintained.

Sententia (sen TEN ti a; L. "judgment, sentiment, opinion") —
Proverb, *q.v.*; **Sage Sayer.** *Also* **Apothegm; Gnome; Maxim;
Aphorism; Adage.** A short pithy statement of a general truth.
See also **Paroemia.**

Sermocinatio (ser mo ci NA ti o; L. "conversation, discussion").
A form of **Prosopopoeia** in which the speaker answers the remarks or questions of a pretended interlocutor: "If anyone asks
why I came, I will tell them the truth — to rob this bank." *See also*
Dialogismus; Hypophora.

Sermo Superfluus (SER MO SU PER flu us) — **Macrologia.**

Sermo Ubique Sui Similis (SER MO u BI que   su i   SIM i lis; L.
"repetitive discourse") — **Homiologia.**

Significatio (sig nif i CA ti o; L. "sign"). To imply more than one
says: an innuendo. *See also* **Emphasis; Syllogismus.**

Silence. Puttenham's term for **Aposiopesis.**

Simile (L. "like") — **Similitude.** *See* **Metaphor.** One thing is likened to another, dissimilar thing by the use of *like, as,* etc.; distinguished from metaphor in that the comparison is made explicit: "My love is like a red, red rose." From Aristotle onward, **Simile** is often the vehicle for **Icon** or **Imago,** *q.v.*

Simile Casibus (SIM i le   CAS i bus; L. "alike in case") — **Homoioptoton.**

Simile Determinatione (SIM i le   de ter min a ti o ne; L. "alike in ending") — **Homoioteleuton.**

Similiter Cadens (si MIL i ter   CA dens; L. "closing or falling alike").

1. **Homoioptoton.**
2. Closing with the same **Cursus,** *q.v.*

Similiter Desinens (DE si nens; L. "ending alike") — **Homoioteleuton.**

Similitude; alt. sp. **Similitudo** — **Simile.**

Single Supply. Puttenham's term for **Zeugma.**

Skesis (SKE sis) — **Paronomasia.**

Slowe Returne. Puttenham's term for **Epanalepsis.**

Solecismus (so le CIS mus; G. "speaking incorrectly") — **Incongruitie.** Ignorant misuse of cases, genders, and tenses. *See* **Malapropism.**

Soother. Puttenham's term for **Euphemismus** (2).

Soriasmus (sor i AS mus; G. "heaping up") — **Cumulatio; Mingle Mangle.** Mingling of languages ignorantly or affectedly. *See also* **Cacozelia:**

> "Most barbarous intimation! yet a kind of insinuation, as it were, in via, in way, of explication; facere, as it were, replication, or rather, ostentare, to show, as it were, his inclination, after his undressed, unpolished, uneducated, unpruned, untrained, or rather, unlettered, or ratherest, unconfirmed fashion, to insert again my haud credo for a deer."
>
> *(Love's Labour's Lost,* IV, ii)

Sorites (so RIT es; G. "heap"). A chain of **Categorical Syllogisms** abbreviated into an **Enthymeme,** *q.v.,* which can have any number of premises. A fallacious chain of this sort ("the fallacy of the heap") is also sometimes called a sorites.

Speedie Dispatcher. Puttenham's term for **Expeditio.**

Spiritual Level. *See* **Allegory.**

Square of Opposition. The diagram that shows the traditional ways in which propositions may oppose one another.

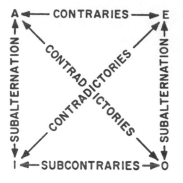

Stasis (STA sis; G. "placing, position") — **Issue.**

Status — Issue.

Stile Coupé. *See* **Senecan Style.**

Stile Serré. *See* **Senecan Style.**

Store. Puttenham's term for **Synonymia.**

Stragler. Puttenham's term for **Parecbasis,** or **Digression,** *q.v.*

Style (L. **Elocutio;** G. **Lexis; Phrasis.**) The third of the five traditional parts of **Rhetoric,** *q.v.*, that which included discussions of the figures used to ornament discourse. Traditionally the most talked-about, if not the most important, part of rhetorical theory. It was by the Ramist theorists maintained to be, with memory and delivery, the *only* part of rhetoric, properly construed; invention and arrangement were thought part of logic. Traditionally, those who have taken the narrower view of rhetoric as a collection of ornamental techniques have naturally emphasized style over the first two parts, and have tended to define the good style as the artificial one, the one as far as possible from everyday usage. See chapter 2.

Subcontraries. Two propositions are subcontraries when they both cannot be false, though both may be true:

Some rubies are valuable.

Some rubies are not valuable.

Subjectio (sub JEC ti o). The questioner suggests the answer to his own question. *See also* **Prosapodosis.** See example under **Hypophora.**

Subsannatio (sub san NA ti o; L. "mockery by gesture") — **Mycterismus.**

Substitute. Puttenham's term for **Hypozeuxis.**

Sufficient Cause. A cause in the presence of which a result must happen.

Sugchrisis; alt. sp. Sygchrisis, Syncrisis.

Superabundancia — Pleonasmus.

Superlatio — Hyperbole.

Surclose. Puttenham's term for **Epiphonema.**

Surnamer. Puttenham's term for **Antonomasia.**

Swift Repeate. Puttenham's term for **Ploce.**

Sygchrisis (SYG chri sis; G. "comparison"); alt. sp **Syncrisis.**

Syllepsis (syl LEP sis; G. "taking together") — **Double Supply.** One verb lacking congruence with at least one subject that it governs: "The Nobles and the King was taken." This device can easily be used as a pun. It differs from zeugma in that zeugma has no faulty congruence. *See* **Zeugma.**

Syllogism. *See* **Categorical Syllogism; Hypothetical Syllogism; Disjunctive Syllogism.**

Syllogismus. Intimation; hinting at something. *See also* **Significatio.** Hamlet describes it in pledging Horatio to secrecy:
> "Here, as before, never, so help you mercy,
> How strange or odd soe'er I bear myself,
> As I perchance hereafter shall think meet
> To put an antic disposition on,
> That you, at such times seeing me, never shall,
> With arms encumber'd thus, or this head-shake,
> Or by pronouncing of some doubtful phrase,
> As 'Well, well, we know,' or 'We could, an if we would,'
> Or 'If we list to speak,' or 'There be, and if they might,'
> Or such ambiguous giving out, to note
> That you know aught of me: this not to do,
> So grace and mercy at your most need help you,
> Swear."

(Hamlet, I, iv)

Symphoresis (sym phor E sis; G. "bringing together") — **Synathroesmus.**

Symploce (SYM plo ce; G. "intertwining") — **Comprehension; Complexio; Conexum; Replie; Koinotes.** *See also* **Conduplicatio.** Repetition of one word or phrase at the beginning, and of an-

other at the end, of successive clauses, sentences, or passages;
a combination of **Anaphora** and **Epistrophe:**

> "Most true that I must fair Fidessa love,
> Most true that fair Fidessa cannot love.
> Most true that I do feel the pains of love,
> Most true that I am captive unto love.
> Most true that I deluded am with love,
> Most true that I do find the sleights of love.
> Most true that nothing can procure her love,
> Most true that I must perish in my love.
> Most true that she contemns the god of love,
> Most true that he is snared with her love.
> Most true that she would have me cease to love,
> Most true that she herself alone is Love.
> Most true that though she hated I would love,
> Most true that dearest life shall end with love."
>
> (Bartholomew Griffin, *Fidessa*, LXII)

Synaeresis (sy NAER e sis; G. "taking or drawing together").
Shortening two syllables to one. We do it twice when we pro-
nounce "Chomondelay" as "Chumley."

Synalepha (syn a LEPH a; G. "to smear or melt together"); alt. sp.
Synaloepha.

1. First of two adjacent vowels is elided; "t'attain" for "to
   attain."
2. One of two adjacent vowels is elided; or rather, the two
   vowels are fused into one.

Synathroesmus (syn a THROE smus; G. "collection, union") —
Frequentatio; Conductio; Heaping Figure.

1. **Congeries** or word heaps.
   > "Who can be wise, amaz'd, temperate and furious,
   > Loyal and neutral, in a moment?"
   >
   > (*Macbeth*, II, iii)

2. **Accumulatio.**

Quintilian points out this difference: "This passage [an example
of accumulatio] recalls the figure styled *Synathroesmus* by the
Greeks, but in that figure it is a number of different things that
are accumulated, whereas in this passage all the accumulated details have but one reference" (VIII, iv, 27).

Synchisis (SYN chis is; G. "to mingle, confuse"). Confused word
order in a sentence:

> "Thine, O then, said the gentle *Redcrosse* knight,
>   Next to that Ladies loue, shalbe the place,
>   O fairest virgin, full of heauenly light."
>   (Spenser, *Faerie Queene*, I, ix, 17)

Synchoresis (syn chor E sis; G. "consent, agreement"). The speaker gives his questioner leave to judge him. *See also* **Concessio.** So Falstaff, in the play-within-a-play in *I Henry IV* (II, iv) says to his tavern audience, "And here I stand: judge, my masters."

Syncope (SYN co pe; G. "cutting [short]"). Letter(s) or syllable(s) removed from the middle of a word: "Inomy" for "ignomy"; "heartly" for "heartily."

Syncrisis (SYN cri sis; G. "comparison, combination"); alt. sp. **Sygchrisis — Dissimilitude.** Comparing contrary elements in contrasting clauses:

> "Cowards die many times before their deaths;
>   The valiant never taste of death but once."
>   (*Julius Caesar*, II, ii)

A kind of **Antithesis,** *q.v.*

Synecdoche (sy NEC do che; G. "understanding one thing with another") — **Intellectio; Quick Conceite.** *See also* **Metonymy.** Substitution of part for whole, genus for species, or vice versa: "All hands on deck."

Syngnome (SYN gno me; G. "fellow-feeling, forbearance"). Forgiveness of injuries.

Synoeciosis (syn oe ci o sis; G. "to associate"), alt. sp. **Synaccensis — Conciliatio; Crosse-Couple.** An expanded **Oxymoron;** a **Paradox.**

Synonymia (syn o NYM i a) — **Communio; Store.** Amplification by synonym:

> "What is become of that beautiful face,
>   Those lovely looks, that favor amiable,
>   Those sweet features, and visage full of grace,
>   That countenance which is alonly able
>   To kill and cure?"
>   (Puttenham)

Synthesis. *See* **Composition.**

Synzeugmenon (syn ZEUG men on; G. "yoked together") — **Zeugma.**

Systole (SYS to le; G. "to draw together, contract") — **Contrac-**

tio. Shortening a naturally long vowel or syllable; opposite of **Diastole.**

Systrophe (SYS tro phe; G. "collection") — **Conglobatio.** Heaping up of descriptions of a thing without defining it:

> "Man is the example of imbecility, the image of unconstancy, the spoil of time, the bondman of misery, the vessel of insatiable desire, and the confident castle of sudden ruin."
>
> (Peacham)

Tapinosis (tap i NO sis; G. "reduction; humiliation; lowness of style") — **Humilatio; Abbaser.** Undignified language that debases a person or thing: "rhymester" for "poet," "verses" for "poetry."

Tasis (TA sis; G. "pitch"). "Sweet and pleasant modulation or tunableness of the voice in pronunciation . . . not precisely a figure" (Sister Miriam Joseph, *Shakespeare's Use of the Arts of Language*, pp. 53–54).

Tautologia (taut o LO gi a; G. "saying the same things") — **Pleonasmus; Circumlocution; Selfe Saying;** inter alia. Repetition of the same idea in different words:

> "LEPIDUS: What manner o'thing is your crocodile?
> ANTONY: It is shap'd, sir, like itself, and it is as broad
>   as it has breadth. It is just so high as it is, and
>   moves with its own organs. It lives by that
>   which nourisheth it, and the elements once
>   out of it, it transmigrates.
> LEPIDUS: What colour is it of?
> ANTONY: Of its own colour too.
> LEPIDUS: 'Tis a strange serpent.
> ANTONY: 'Tis so. And the tears of it are wet."
>
> (*Antony and Cleopatra*, II, vii)

Taxis (TAX is; G. "arrangement, order") — **Arrangement.** Peacham makes it a figure: "Distributes to every subject his most proper and natural adjunct." Touchstone says:

> "As the ox hath his bow, sir, the horse his curb,
> and the falcon her bells, so man hath his desires;
> and as pigeons bill, so wedlock would be nibbling."
>
> (*As You Like It*, III, iii)

Tell Cause. Puttenham's term for **Aetiologia.**

Tenuitas (te NU i tas; L. "fineness, smallness, tenuity") — **Litotes.**

Testamentum (test a MENT um; L. "will; something acknowledged before witnesses"). When not used literally, may mean **Diatyposis.**

Testatio (tes TA ti o; L. "a bearing witness") — **Martyria.**

Thaumasmus (thau MAS mus; G. "marvelling") — **Admiratio.** Exclamation of wonder:

"O, wonder!
How many goodly creatures are there here!
How beauteous mankind is! O brave new world,
That has such people in't!"

(*Tempest*, V, i)

Thesis. One of the two categories into which the Greek rhetorician Hermagoras of Temnos divided the subject of rhetoric: this was a general subject, i.e., "Are mothers-in-law offensive?" The opposite category was **Hypothesis,** *q.v.* Quintilian refers to a thesis as a commonplace (*see* 2.3.7.) in which the "general character of a commonplace is usually given a special turn" (II, iv, 22). Quintilian's word for thesis was "question," and he maintains that Cicero used still another word, "proposition." The thesis was a *definite* question; the hypothesis, an *indefinite* question.

Threnos (THRE nos; G. "dirge"); alt. sp. **Threnody** — **Lamentatio.** A lamentation, Shakespeare's *The Phoenix and the Turtle*, for example.

Tmesis ([t]ME sis; G. "a cutting") — **Diacope** (1).

Ton Kairon (kai RON). The Greek phrase for time, place, circumstances of a subject. Gorgias maintained that since there was no absolute truth, two antithetical statements could be made on any subject: only by reference to ton kairon could one decide which side to take.

Tolerantia (tol e RAN ti a; L. "endurance") — **Apocarteresis.**

Too Full Speech. Puttenham's term for **Pleonasmus.**

Topics (*topoi*). The topics were for Aristotle, as they have been for rhetoricians since, both the stuff of which arguments are made and the form of those arguments. Neither Aristotle nor those theorists following him always made it clear with which aspect they were concerned. The twenty-eight valid and ten fallacious topics listed in sections 2.3.4. and 2.3.5. are formal rather than material; they are the traditional topics. Aristotle distinguished them, general topics applicable to all subjects alike, from those that could be applied only to a specific subject or question. The long list of topics is often shortened to basic types: genus and species, nature, authority, consequence, time and place, word, etc. Later, more general usage has confused the topics with the *loci communes* or commonplace observations or literary situations; both are part of that planned spontaneity which was an orator's principal means of dazzling his audience.

Topographia (top o GRAPH i a). Type of **Energia:** description of places. *See also* **Prosopographia; Chorographia; Chronographia; Geographia; Hydrographia; Anemographia; Dendrographia; Counterfait Place.**

Topothesia (top o THES i a; G. "description of a place") — **Loci Positio.** Description of imaginary, nonexistent places.

To Prepon (to PREP on; G. "what is fitting") — **Decorum.**

Traductio (tra DUC ti o; L. "leading along; a transferring or metonymy; repetition of a word").

    1. **Ploce; Translacer.**
    2. **Polyptoton.**

Traiectio in Alium (tra IEC ti o in AL ium; L. "pushing onto another"). Shifting of responsibility. Henry V to the Archbishop of Canterbury:

> "For God doth know how many now in health
> Shall drop their blood in approbation
> Of what your reverence shall incite us to."
> *(Henry V,* I, ii)

Transcensio (trans CEN si o; L. "climbing over") — **Hyperbaton.**

Transgressio (trans GRESS i o; L. "going across") — **Hyperbaton.**

Transiectio (trans IEC ti o; L. "passing over") — **Hyperbaton.**

Transitio (tran SIT i o; L. "going across or over") — **Metabasis.**

Translacer. Puttenham's term for **Traductio.**

Translatio (trans LA ti o; L. "transferring") — **Metaphor.**

Transmotio (trans MO ti o; L. "transposing") — **Metastasis.**

Transmutation — **Metonymy.**

Transnominatio (trans no min A ti o) — **Metonymy.**

Transplacement — **Antanaclasis.**

Transport. Puttenham's term for **Metaphor.**

Transposition — **Antisthecon; Metathesis.**

Transumptio (tran SUMP ti o; L. "assuming one thing for another") — **Metalepsis.**

Trespasser. Puttenham's term for **Hyperbaton.**

Trivium (TRIV i um; L. "an intersection of three roads"). The traditional medieval curriculum leading to the B.A. It was composed of grammar, logic, and rhetoric. Together with the **Quad-rivium,** *q.v.,* it comprised the seven liberal arts.

Trope (G. "a turn") — **Turn.** Theorists have differed in defining this term, and any single definition would be prescriptive. Such consensus as there is wants trope to mean a figure that changes the meaning of a word or words, rather than simply arranging them in a pattern of some sort. (Thus the distinction would roughly correspond to that between true and false wit in the time of Pope.) That the placing of a word in a highly artificial pattern — a **Scheme,** *q.v.* — usually involves some change of its meaning is a point theorists have more often ignored than quarreled over. Cicero would like trope to be used for changes in meaning of one word only; for more than one word, use **Figure.** Quintilian, on the other hand, points out that the kind of change in meaning involved occurs on a larger scale than in single words, and that the *change in signification* is the crucial issue. Bede agrees, defining trope as a change from its normal significance of any utterance (*dictio*). For Quintilian, a figure is a form or pattern of speech or writing which differs from the ordinary. So, we might say that, for him, a trope is a change in meaning, a figure is a change in form. (In Book I, he divides the figures [*schemata*] into figures of speech [*lexeos*] and figures of thought [*dianoias*]. The use of these terms seems to me by no means clear in Books VIII and IX, especially in VIII, vi, 40, where the whole distinction seems to collapse. The student who wishes to pursue the matter might well begin with the opening discussion of IX.) Still another related set of categories is presented in Fortunatianus' *Ars* (Halm). Figures are divided into three types: (1) *lexeos* — of one word; (2) *logou* — of more than one word; (3) *dianoias* — of thought, in whatever form. The central problem — when does a change in meaning become a change in thought? — obscures his further distinction of figures into figures of thought (*dianoias*) and figures of words (*lexeos*).

Two fundamental distinctions seem to wander through the considerable theoretical disagreement: (1) changes in form and changes in meaning; (2) the size or scope of the change. I have tried to preserve these two distinctions as simply as possible in the categorical and descriptive lists that appear in the following chapters. Scholars have used this cluster of terms with a confidence that is belied by the primary disagreement about them. I have tried to outline such consistency as I could see.

The issues involved seem complex enough to preclude an adequate distinction. The body of opinion which makes trope a truly metaphorical change in a word's use, a change in meaning, and scheme a superficial or merely decorative change, really took hold in modern theorizing — so far as I can trace it — with the work of the late Morris W. Croll. (The classical distinction would seem to be largely an Augustan one.) Croll used all his terms with authority, but his use of them might trouble modern students more than it does. Jonas Barish ("The Prose Style of John Lyly," *ELH*, XXIII [March, 1956]) has pointed out the problems a rigid trope-scheme distinction creates:

> "On the whole, a contemporary reader is likely to be disturbed by the earnestness with which Croll propounds the Renaissance distinction between "figures of thought" (tropes) and "figures of sound" (schemes). The distinction, which drives a wedge between style and content, and treats them as though they enjoyed separate and independent existence, if it interferes even with objective descriptions of style, interferes still more with any effort to get at the heart of a writer's artistic universe where style and meaning interpenetrate."

And at more than one point in *The Senecan Amble*, Williamson shows how the same figure is (metaphorical) trope in one writer and (ornamental) scheme in another.

It is easy enough, once you have a list of ornaments clearly divided between easy and difficult, sound and thought, trope and scheme (see Atkins' breakdown, given in chap. 4), to characterize, or castigate, an author for using the easy figures, or the schemes, rather than the difficult figures, or the tropes. But it is by no means clear that such a predetermined division will do justice to any particular text, especially to a literary one. Take a simple example. Hyperbaton, a generic term for departure from ordinary word order, is a trope according to Atkins' summary. Yet under it we must group several of the figures of words (**Anaphora, Conduplicatio, Ploce, Compar**), since they clearly depend on an "unnatural" word order, the kind Lyly favored and was reproached for. The distinction immediately breaks down, of course, because "natural" is impossible to define. What is "natural" for *Euphues* or Sidney's *Arcadia* is hardly the word order of everyday speech. The point to be taken is that the trope-scheme distinction contains a hidden premise of "naturalness" which may be unacceptable to a literary critic.

Take a more complex example. Euphues, at the beginning of *Euphues*, is answering a Polonius-like warning about the evils that may befall him, by playing elaborately on the word "nature":

> "Now whereas you seem to love my nature, & loathe
> my nurture, you bewray your own weakness, in think-
> ing that nature may anyways be altered by education,
> & as you have ensamples to confirm your pretence, so
> I have most evident and infallible arguments to serve
> for my purpose: It is natural for the vine to spread.
> . . . It is proper . . ."

These are schemes, easy ornaments (**Ploce** and **Polyptoton** and withal a **Paronomasia** on "nurture"). Yet the whole passage (of which I have quoted only the beginning) is radically metaphorical, aims to redefine both "nature" and "nurture." Further, both redefinitions are argumentative techniques, and the kind of persuasion they are meant to effect (their "naturalness," their rhetorical decorum) will depend on a full understanding of the dramatic context. Such an understanding here yields the conclusion that the real subject of the passage is neither "nature" nor "nurture" but wit. Euphues' real argument is that his wit is deep enough to avoid the dangers so fully foreseen for him. The passage must then finally be described as a hyperbolic periphrasis that builds a complex and ironical metaphor for wit. **Hyperbole, Periphrasis,** and **Metaphor** are all tropes, of course.

The historian of rhetoric will want to preserve all the distinctions that have been made. But it seems a doubtful wisdom for the literary critic to restrict himself to categories inadequate to describe all but the simplest literary texts.

Tropological Level. *See* **Allegory.**

Turn. The English term for **Trope**, *q.v.*; it was widely used in the seventeenth and eighteenth centuries as a general term for a wide range of syntactical figures of speech.

Turne Tale. Puttenham's term for **Apostrophe.**

Turpis Locutio (TUR pis lo CU ti o) — **Cacemphaton.**

Twinnes. Puttenham's term for **Hendyadis.**

Uncouthe. Puttenham's term for **Acyrologia.**

Underlay. Puttenham's term for **Epizeuxis.**

Undistributed Term (of a syllogism). Refers to only a part of class designated by term.

Urbanitas (ur BAN i tas; L. "refinement, delicacy") — **Asteismus.**

Utis (oo tis; G. "no one"). The Nobody Argument: "The Nobody argument is an argument whose major premise consists of an indefinite and definite clause, followed by a minor premise and conclusion: for example, 'If anyone is here, he is not at Rhodes; but there is someone here, therefore there is not anyone in Rhodes' " (Diogenes Laertius, VIII, ["Zeno"]).

Vices of Language. Perhaps it is the counsel of depraved relativism rather than of a golden mean that every vice was once a virtue, but it is clearly the counsel of rhetoricians: therefore no figure is always a vice except those that deliberately say so — and even they may be redeemed. Conversely, any virtue can be viciously used. To divide figures, outside any context, into *vices* and *virtues* seems less foolish than impossible.

Before a modern reader decides that an earlier writer has laid his rhetorical ornament on with a trowel he might often look with profit at the context. No one thinks that Holofernes, in *Love's Labour's Lost,* speaks for Shakespeare, but analogous confusions often pass current where the dramatic context is less immediately clear. In fact, it might be argued that a writer cannot possibly go haywire to the degree that the moralizing way of thinking (which gives us the phrase "vices of language") maintains. If the flowers of rhetoric are so dense as to obscure any kind of denotative meaning, we can only assume that the "meaning" intended is the floral display itself. Surely an age that cut its teeth on symbolist poetry need not be troubled by a presentation of words for their own sake. One step beyond such display puts us, of course, into the treatise or rhetorical diploma-piece category, and again the thing justifies itself. The only test for the arts of rhetoric is effectiveness, not virtue: when a rhetorical pitch calls attention to itself as rhetorical, it does not (*pace* Aristotle, *Rhetoric*, III, 1404^b) necessarily lose its effectiveness. It simply moves over into another, more self-conscious kind of appeal, one where the rules of the game are different. *See* **Euphuism.**

Vision — **Demonstratio.**

Votum (vo tum; L. "vow") — **Euche.**

Wondrer. Puttenham's term for **Paradox.**

Zeugma (ZEUG ma; G. "yoking") — **Single Supply; Synzeugmen-**

on. One verb governs several congruent words or clauses, each in a different way; as in *The Rape of the Lock*:

"Here thou, great *Anna!* whom three realms obey,
Dost sometimes counsel take — and sometimes Tea."

The term **Hyperzeugma** is sometimes used even when every object in a series has its own verb or preposition. *See* **Prozeugma; Mezozeugma; Hypozeugma; Epezeugmenon; Syllepsis.**

2.

TERMS CLASSIFIED ACCORDING TO DIVISIONS OF RHETORIC

2.1. Rhetoric: The five parts

Invention	(L. *inventio*)	(G. *heuresis*)
Arrangement	(L. *dispositio*)	(G. *taxis*)
Style	(L. *elocutio*)	(G. *lexis*)
Memory	(L. *memoria*)	(G. *mneme*)
Delivery	(L. *actio*)	(G. *hypocrisis*)

"All the activity and ability of an orator falls into five divisions. . . . He must first hit upon what to say; then manage and marshal his discoveries, not merely in orderly fashion, but with a discriminating eye for the exact weight as it were of each argument; next go on to array them in the adornments of style; after that keep them guarded in his memory; and in the end deliver them with effect and charm." (Cicero, *De Oratore*, I, xxxi, 142–143.)

The Ramists (*see* **Rhetoric**) would reduce these five parts to two, Style and Delivery, giving Invention and Arrangement to Logic, and leaving out Memory altogether, as a subsidiary classification.

2.2. Rhetoric: The three branches

Deliberative (to exhort or dissuade; L. *genus deliberativum*; G. *genos symbouleutikon*).

Judicial (forensic; to accuse or defend; L. *genus iudiciale*; G. *genos dikanikon*).

Epideictic or Panegyric (to blame or commemorate; L. *genus demonstrativum*; G. *genos epideiktikon* or *panegyrikon*).

(These correspond to the traditional three types of arguments.)

2.3.1. Invention: Two kinds of proof, after Aristotle's *Rhetoric*
1. Inartificial Proof: All that today would be called "evi-

dence" — sworn testimony, documents, scientific analyses, laws.
   2. Artificial Proof: Three main types.
      a. Establishing the persuader's good character and hence credibility. This is called **Ethos.**
      b. Putting the audience in an acceptable mood, by playing on its feelings. This is called **Pathos.**
      c. Proving, or seeming to prove, the case. The plainest term for this is rational argument or **Logos** (*Logic*).

2.3.2. Invention: Two types of logical proof
   1. Deductive
      a. If the premises are scientifically demonstrated, the term for the argument is **Syllogism.**
      b. If the premises are only probably true, the term for the argument is **Enthymeme.** (Enthymemes are either demonstrative or refutative.) This is the more common form in rhetoric.
   2. Inductive
      a. If all instances of the phenomenon are accounted for, the induction is *scientific.*
      b. If only selected instances are cited, the argument is from *example.* This is the more common form in rhetoric.

2.3.3. Invention: Two kinds of topics (*topoi*), after Aristotle's *Rhetoric*
   1. Topics useful in a special area of knowledge only (*idioi topoi*).
   2. Topics useful in arguments of all kinds (*koinoi topoi*). Four main ones are given:
      a. What can and cannot happen.
      b. What has and has not happened.
      c. What will or will not happen.
      d. Size.
At another point in the *Rhetoric*, Aristotle introduces twenty-eight valid and ten invalid topics useful in devising enthymemes. They follow.

2.3.4. Invention: Twenty-eight valid topics, after Aristotle's *Rhetoric*
   1. Restate your contention in an opposite way: e.g., instead

of "excess is bad," say "Moderation is good." If the opposite statement holds, so will the original one.

2. Redefine a key term slightly to support your contention, or suggest a synonym that seems better to support it.

3. Use a correlative idea. You want to prove B justly punished, so prove A just in punishing him.

4. A fortiori argument. If you want to prove A has acted in a cruel way at one time, show that at another he acted still more cruelly.

5. Argue from circumstances of past time. What has been promised at one time must be performed at another, even though times and circumstances may have changed.

6. Turn an accusation against the accuser. The implied moral superiority of the accuser is thus attacked. The topic will not work if the accusation is obviously just, since if you do something, you cannot effectively reproach others for doing the same thing.

7. Define your terms so as to place the argument in a favorable light.

8. Play upon various senses of a word.

9. Divide your argument into its logical parts.

10. Argue from plain induction (parallel cases).

11. Argue from authority or previous verdict.

12. Argue your contention part by part.

13. Argue from consequences, good or bad.

14. When an action may have good or bad consequences, invert your opponent's arguments. Aristotle's example: Don't take up oratory. If you say truth, men will hate you; if you lie, the gods will hate you. Take up oratory. If you lie, men will love you; if you say the truth, the gods will love you. (Variation of 13.)

15. Oppose an argument by seeming to allow it and then maintaining that things are not what they seem. If the opponent maintains thus, argue things *are* what they seem.

16. Argue from logical consequences. If a man is old enough to fight for his country, he is old enough to vote. Are we then to say that those too sick to fight should not vote?

17. Argue that if two results are the same, their causes must be the same.

18. Apply an opponent's earlier decision to a later case, to his disadvantage.
19. Take the possible motive for the one actually prevailing.
20. In arguing individual motive, point to general motives or prohibitions (for or against, depending on which side you have taken).
21. Make people believe an improbability by pointing to an even greater one that is yet true.
22. Catch your opponent out on inaccuracies and self-contradictions.
23. Refute slander by showing that it was evoked by a mistaken view of the facts.
24. Prove effect by showing the presence of its cause, or vice versa.
25. Show that a client or a cause had a better argument and failed to use it. Only trustful innocence would make such a mistake.
26. Disprove an action by showing it inconsistent with previous actions.
27. Use previous mistakes as a defense (or explanation) for present ones.
28. Support an argument by playing upon the meaning of names. For example, "Mr. Stern is a harsh man."

The common reduction of these topics for the purpose of prose exposition are the arguments from time, analogy, cause and effect, class, comparison, etc.

2.3.5. Invention: Ten invalid topics or fallacies of arguments, after Aristotle's *Rhetoric*

1. Conclude an argument, as if at the end of a reasoning process, without having gone through the process.
2. Play on illogical, fortuitous similarity of words. (A saucepan must be noble for so was the great god Pan.)
3. Make a statement about the whole, true only of individual parts, or vice versa.
4. Use indignant language.
5. Use a single, unrepresentative example.
6. Take the accidental as essential.
7. Argue from consequence.
8. Argue *post hoc, propter hoc*.
9. Ignore crucial circumstances.

10. Make out, from fraudulent confusion of general and particular, that the improbable is probable, and vice versa.

2.3.6. Invention: Sixteen basic topics, after Cicero's *Topica*
1. Argument from definition.
2. Argument from partition.
3. Argument based on etymology.
4. Argument based on conjugates.
5. Argument derived from genus.
6. Argument derived from species.
7. Argument based on similarity or analogy.
8. Argument based on difference.
9. Argument from contraries.
10. Argument from adjuncts.
11. Argument from antecedents.
12. Argument from consequents.
13. Argument from contradictions.
14. Argument from efficient cause.
15. Argument from effects.
16. Argument from comparison.

2.3.7. Invention: The Commonplaces (L. *loci communes*; G. *koinoi topoi*)

The term is a vague one, and the category so large as to prohibit enumeration. A commonplace was a general argument, observation, or description a speaker could memorize for use on any number of possible occasions. So an American statesman who knows he will be asked to speak extempore on the Fourth of July might commit to memory descriptions of Jefferson's face, of the building of the Capitol, tags from the Declaration of Independence, praise of famous American victories. A few scattered traditional *loci*: death is common to all; time flies; the contemplative vs. the active life; a soldier's career vs. scholar's; praise of a place as paradisiacal; the uses of the past; a short, celebrated life vs. a long, obscure one. The commonplace is the general term for, or at least overlaps, the device Aristotle defined more narrowly, and placed specifically in the definition of Invention, in the lists above. Thus *loci*, properly speaking, has two overlapping meanings: commonplace observations, and common sources of arguments. Collections of rhetorical commonplaces, of whatever sort, have always been surveys, as Kenneth Burke writes in blending the two meanings, "of the things that people generally consider persuasive, and of methods that have persuasive effects" (*Rhetoric of Motives*, p. 580).

Or, as Pope humorously described them in the *Peri Bathous*: "I therefore propose that there be contrived with all convenient dispatch, at the public expense, a *Rhetorical Chest of Drawers*, consisting of three Stories, the highest for the *Deliberative*, the middle for the *Demonstrative*, and the lowest for the *Judicial*. These shall be divided into *Loci*, or *Places*, being repositories for Matter and Argument in the several kinds of oration or writing." (For an illuminating discussion of literary use of commonplaces, see Rosemond Tuve, *Elizabethan and Metaphysical Imagery*, pp. 284 ff.) Modern persuasive techniques have tended to make much less use of the commonplaces than did earlier periods largely, as Howell makes clear (*Logic and Rhetoric in England*, pp. 23–24, and elsewhere), because we no longer trust traditional wisdom, are far more interested in investigating the world anew. *See* **Proof.**

2.3.8. Invention: The main points at issue

Stasis is the Greek term for the main point at issue in a legal argument (the Latin term is *constitutio*); who has done what, when, and how. Some theorists further narrow the definition to the starting point of a case — the circumstances that give rise to it — or to the first point raised by an opponent in a legal case. (For fuller discussion see **Issue**).

2.3.9. Invention: Thesis and hypothesis (general and particular arguments), after Hermagoras

Hermagoras divided political questions into two types:
1. Thesis: a general argument, one that does not deal with particular cases (L. *questio*).
2. Hypothesis: argument about a particular case (L. *causa*).
   Its two subdivisions:
   a. Question of fact or justice
   b. Question of law
   Its seven elements:
   a. Actor
   b. Action
   c. Time
   d. Place

    e. Cause
    f. Manner
    g. Starting point.

2.4. Arrangement: The seven parts of an oration
  1. Entrance or Prooemium (*exordium*) — catches the audience's attention.
  2. Narration (*praecognitio* or *narratio*) — sets forth the facts.
  3. Exposition or Definition (*explicatio* or *definitio*) — defines terms and opens issues to be proved.
  4. Proposition (*partitio*) — clarifies the points at issue; states exactly what is to be proved.
  5. Confirmation (*amplificatio*)— sets forth the arguments for and against; proof.
  6. Confutation or Refutation (*refutatio* or *reprehensio*) — refutes opponent's arguments.
  7. Conclusion or Epilogue (*peroratio* or *epilogus*) — sums up arguments and stirs audience.

Various theorists reduce the number of parts. Aristotle sees two essential elements, the statement of the issue (Exposition) and the arguments for and against (Confirmation). At most, he thought, an Entrance and Conclusion framing the two essential parts would make a total of four. Cicero, in *De Inventione* (Book I contains a full discussion of each of the parts), and the author of *Rhetorica ad Herennium*, combine numbers three and four above, Cicero adding a Digression before the Conclusion. Cicero tells us that Hermagoras sometimes inserted an Amplification after the Confirmation. The Proposition was sometimes divided into Primary (about things) and Secondary (about other propositions). Numbers 3–6 can be grouped as proof (*probatio*). The only principle governing the number of divisions used would seem to be the nature of the speech (whether it was deliberative, judicial, or epideictic), and the circumstances of presentation.

    Although extensively discussed in its component details, the form of the oration has not received the scholarly attention it deserves, as the form that has governed a good deal of writing and speaking not specifically rhetorical. Its structure has influenced the way we think and argue, of course, in every instance where we argue a case. Thus we always try to establish a specific controllable relation to an audience, always *seem* to take our opponent's arguments into account (paraphrase his weak ones, distort his strong ones), always dilate our own good reasons, always offer a loaded summary before we stop. The ingredients of the form, then, vary considerably, but the form itself is used, albeit unknowingly, by an enormous number of people.

Beyond its rhetorical use, it often can be detected, writ large, where the argumentative element is secondary. We tend to take it as an inevitable pattern of dialectic thought. In fact, there seems no more reason to regard it as an inevitable form for an argument than there does to regard beginning-middle-end as the only form for a narrative. Its primary assumption, for example, is that all arguments are or can be polar opposites (the *dialectic* assumption, odd as this seems), and it does violence to any issue that falls into the "both-and" rather than the "either-or" category. It can offer a form for argument, that is, but not for compromise. How many compromises, it is then reasonable to ask, have been hindered by the *form*?

2.5.1. Style: The three types
1. The Low or Plain Style (*genus humile*, or *extenuatum*).
2. The Middle Style (*genus medium*, or *modicum*, or *mediocre*, or *temperatum*).
3. The Grand Style (*genus grande*, or *grave*).

An analogous, but not identical, set of categories often found:
1. The Attic, or unornamented, brief style,
2. The Asiatic, or ornamented, full style.
3. The Rhodian, somewhere between 1 and 2.

The Greek critic Demetrius, in *On Style*, offers a fourfold division:
1. Plain
2. Grand
3. Elegant
4. Forceful

One modern scholar of rhetoric has maintained that two fundamental styles existed in Greece from the earliest times. If so, this two-part division provided the first categorization of style in western Europe. The three-part division has been by far the most common, however; largely, one may suspect, because it is so vague. This division, one can say very generally, has been made on the basis of one or more of the following: (*a*) subject (generally, the more important the topic, the higher the style); (*b*) diction (presence or absence of figurative language); (*c*) effect on the audience (the grand style had the greatest emotional effect); (*d*) syntax or composition (the grand style was made up of balanced elements in intricate arrangements; the plain style used shorter periods, followed more closely the processes of discursive thought). The High, Middle, and Low styles each have defective counterparts: the Swollen, the Loose (*dissolutum*), the Meager.

Kenneth Burke (*Rhetoric of Motives*, pp. 597–598) suggests, as a Ciceronian paraphrase, the following rationale for the three levels of style:

> "In his *Orator*, an earlier work than the *De Oratore*, . . . Cicero distinguishes three styles (*genera dicendi*, *genera scribendi*): the grandiloquent, plain, tempered. And he names the three 'offices' of the orator: (1) to teach, inform, instruct (*docere*); (2) to please (*delectare*); (3) to move or 'bend' (*movere*, *flectere*). He also refers to styles in a more personal or individual sense, when observing that orators are next of kin to poets, and that each poet has his own way of writing (and in a critical digression he gives a catalogue of formulas for succinctly characterizing and savoring the distinctive qualities in the personal style of various writers well known to antiquity). However, the three over-all styles of oratory are not thought of thus, as personal expression, but as a means for carrying out the three 'offices.' That is, the plain style is best for teaching, the tempered style for pleasing, and the ornate (grandiloquent) style for moving. Though human weakness makes an orator more able in one or another of these styles, the ideal orator should be master of all three, since an oration aims at all three functions."

It might also be possible to use as metaphor not "level" but "spectrum." We might, for example, place styles on a spectrum of opacity. At one extreme would be a style like Lyly's in *Euphues*, an extremely opaque style that we are to notice as stylistic surface. We do not, that is, condemn it for hiding a clear prose meaning — a plain narrative — behind it, because there is none behind it. Such meaning as it creates comes from the stylistic surface. To galvanize a modern critical cliche, the style is the meaning. At the other end of such a spectrum, the aim would be translucence, the purely denotative style of Bishop Sprat's desire. At this extreme, the style would be pure means to describe event. At the opposite end, style would be itself the event. A way of bending the spectrum into a circle might be found by trying to place a prose like Hemingway's on it. Such a style, which continually calls attention to itself by its mannerisms but whose mannerisms all aim to create the effect of an extremely denotative translucent prose, nothing but the facts, would seem to partake of both ends of the spectrum. In other words, such a style would suggest that the degree of ornament of a style and the self-consciousness of a style are not the same thing. Two further categories would then seem to be possible: the style (plain or ornate) which acknowledges that it is a style, a rhetoric, an effort at persuasion, and the style (plain or ornate) which does not. The final conclusion that this train of reasoning suggests is this: as an addition to the classical categories of style — based on the degree of ornament, largely — we might categorize on the basis of the degree of self-consciousness with which the style presents itself.

2.5.2. Style: The four virtues

Theophrastus, in his lost *On Style*, isolated four virtues, which Cicero used in the *De Oratore* as the basis for his discussion of style:
1. Purity (correctness).
2. Clarity.
3. Decorum (G. *to prepon* — that which is fitting to time, place, etc.).
4. Ornament.

The *Rhetorica ad Herennium* offers three categories:
1. *Elegantia*
   a. *latinitas* (correctness, good Latin).
   b. *explanatio* (clarity).
2. *Compositio* (avoiding harsh sound clashes and excessively figured language; making the style uniformly polished). Quintilian offers a threefold division: "Style has three kinds of excellence, correctness, lucidity, and elegance (for many include the all-important quality of appropriateness under the heading of elegance)."

3. *Dignitas* (embellishment by a variety of figures tastefully used).

In all these schemes, of course, each virtue, like each level of style, has a corresponding vice. A great many other virtues and vices have been suggested; they all seem reducible to the four of Theophrastus.

2.5.3. Style: The Figures

Figure: The term figure in its most general meaning refers to any device or pattern of language in which meaning is changed or enhanced. The term has two subcategories:

1. Figure of words
   a. Trope: use of a word to mean something other than its ordinary meaning — a metaphor, for example.
   b. Scheme: a figure in which words preserve their literal meaning, but are placed in a significant arrangement of some kind.
2. Figure of thought: a large-scale trope or scheme, or a combination of both — allegory, for example.

This categorization is prescriptive (*see* **Trope**). All these terms have been used interchangeably at one time or another to refer to the numerous devices of language which were classified first by the Greek rhetorical theorists and later, in increasing numbers, by the Latin rhetoricians. In the next chapter these devices are arranged into twelve general types. In chapter 4, major terms are given in the more traditional division.

3.

THE TERMS BY TYPE

These lists aim to help a student move from a text to the term that describes it. No accurate, dependable, airtight division into discrete categories exists, to my knowledge, even for the figures alone. (*See* **Trope** for a brief discussion of the problems of the most common trope-scheme division.) This one pretends to nothing except ease of reference to the alphabetical list. The categories overlap, in some instances.

3.1. Addition, Subtraction, and Substitution of Letters and Syllables

antisthecon: substituting one letter or sound for another within a word.

aphaeresis: omitting a syllable from the beginning of a word.

apocope: omitting the last syllable or letter of a word.

diastole: lengthening a syllable or vowel that is usually short.

epenthesis: addition of a letter, sound, or syllable to the middle of a word.

metaplasm: moving from their natural place letters or syllables of a word; generic term that includes most of the words in this section.

metathesis: transposition of letters out of normal order in a word.

paragoge: adding a letter or syllable to the end of a word.

proparalepsis: adding a syllable to the end of a word.

prosthesis: adding a letter or syllable to the beginning of a word.

synaeresis: shortening two syllables to one.

synalepha: eliding first of two adjacent vowels.

syncope: removing letters or syllables from the middle of a word.

systole: shortening a naturally long vowel or syllable.

3.2. Addition, Subtraction, and Substitution of Words, Phrases, and Clauses

anapodoton: omission of a clause from a sentence.

asyndeton: omission of conjunctions between words, phrases, clauses.
diacope: separation of the elements of a compound word by another word or words.
ellipsis: omission of a word easily understood.
hypozeugma: a type of zeugma, *q.v.*, with verb in last clause.
mezozeugma: a type of zeugma, *q.v.*, with verb in middle of construction.
parelcon: addition of superfluous words.
prozeugma: a type of zeugma, *q.v.*, with verb in first clause.
zeugma: use of one word to govern several congruent words or clauses.

3.3. Amplification
aetiologia: giving a cause or reason.
anacephalaeosis: a recapitulation.
apophasis:
   a. all alternatives rejected except one.
   b. pretending to ignore what is really affirmed.
   c. giving many reasons and confuting each.
apoplanesis: evading the issue by digressing.
asiatismus: a style full of figures and words lacking matter.
bomphiologia: bombastic speech.
congeries: word heaps.
continuatio: a long, full sentence.
diaeresis: dividing genus into species in order to amplify.
diallage: bringing several arguments to establish a single point.
digestion: an orderly enumeration of points to be discussed.
distribution: dividing the whole into its parts.
divisio: dividing into kinds or classes.
enumeratio: dividing subjects into adjuncts, causes into effects, antecedents into consequents.
epanodos: expanding a statement by discussing it part by part.
epexegesis: adding words or phrases for amplification.
epitheton: qualifying a subject with an appropriate adjective.
macrologia: long-winded speech.
megaloprepeia: magnificent and elevated utterance.
metanoia: qualifying a statement by recalling it and expressing it in a better way.
parenthesis: a word, phrase, or sentence inserted as an aside.
periphrasis: circumlocution.

peristasis: amplifying by detailing circumstances.
synonymia: amplification by synonym.
systrophe: heaping up descriptions of a thing without defining it.

3.4. Balance, Antithesis, and Paradox

alloiosis: breaking down a subject into alternatives.
antanagoge: balancing an unfavorable aspect with a favorable one.
anthypophora: asking questions and answering them.
anticategoria: mutual accusation or recrimination.
antimetabole: inverting the order of repeated words.
antinomy: comparing one law, or a part of a law, to another.
antiphrasis: irony of one word, calling a "dwarf" a "giant."
antisagoge:

- *a.* assuring a reward to those who possess a virtue, or a punishment to those who hold it in contempt.
- *b.* stating first one side of a proposition, then the other, with equal vigor.

apocrisis: replying to one's own arguments.
apophonema: a sententia put in antithetical form
chiasmus: order of first phrase or clause reversed in second.
climax: mounting by degrees through words or sentences of increasing weight and in parallel construction.
commutatio: order of first clause reversed in second.
contrarium: one of two opposite statements is used to prove the other.
dialysis: arguing from a series of disjunctive propositions.
dilemma: argument that offers an opponent unacceptable choices.
enigma: a riddle.
euphuism: an elaborate prose style that makes use of balance and antithesis.
hypophora: asking questions and answering them.
hypozeuxis: every clause in a sentence has its own subject and verb.
isocolon: a repetition of phrases of equal length and usually corresponding structure.
litotes: denial of the contrary.
oxymoron: a condensed paradox.
paromoiosis: a parallelism of sounds between words of two equal clauses.
polysyndeton: using a conjunction between each clause.

progressio: advancing by steps of comparison.
prosapodosis: supporting each alternative with a reason.
sermocinatio: the speaker answers the remarks or questions of a pretended interlocuter.
syncrisis: comparing contrary elements in contrasting clauses.
synoeciosis: an expanded paradox.
taxis: distributing to every subject its proper adjunct.

3.5. Brevity
brachylogia: brevity of diction.
brevitas: concise expression.
diazeugma: one subject with many verbs.
epiphonema: a striking epigram used for summary.
epitrochasmus: a swift movement from one statement to another.
fable: a short, allegorical story.
hypozeugma: a type of zeugma, *q.v.*, with verb in last clause.
mezozeugma: a type of zeugma, *q.v.*, with verb in middle of construction.
oxymoron: a condensed paradox.
proverb: a short, pithy statement of a general truth. Category includes adage, apothegm, gnome, maxim, sententia.
prozeugma: a type of zeugma, *q.v.*, with verb in first clause.
zeugma: use of one word to govern several congruent words or clauses.

3.6. Description
anatomy: the analysis of an issue into its constituent parts.
anemographia: description of the wind.
characterismus: description of body or mind.
chorographia: description of a nation.
chronographia: description of time.
dendrographia: description of a tree.
effictio: personal description (outward appearance; a head-to-toe catalog).
effiguration: elaborate description of an object or event.
energia: clear, lucid, vivid description; also, generic term for various types of description.
ethopoeia: description of natural propensities.
geographia: description of the earth.
hydrographia: description of water.

hypotyposis: mimicry of acts.
icon: painting resemblance by imagery.
mimesis: imitation of gesture, pronunciation, utterance.
onomatopoeia: use or invention of words that sound like their meaning.
pragmatographia: vivid description of an action or event.
prosopographia: description of imaginary persons or bodies.
topographia: description of places.
topothesia: description of imaginary, nonexistent places.

3.7. Emotional Appeals and Exhortations

amphidiorthosis: to hedge or qualify a charge made in anger.
anacoenosis: asking the opinion of one's readers or hearers.
anticategoria: mutual accusation or recrimination.
antirrhesis: rejecting an argument because of its insignificance, error, or wickedness.
apaetesis: a matter put aside in anger is resumed later.
apocarteresis: casting away all hope in one direction and turning to another for aid.
apodioxis: rejecting an argument indignantly as impertinent or absurdly false.
aporia: true or feigned doubt or deliberation about an issue.
aposiopesis: stopping suddenly in midcourse, leaving a statement unfinished.
apostrophe: breaking off discourse to address directly some present or absent person or thing.
ara: curse or imprecation.
asphalia: one offers oneself as surety for a bond.
bdelygma: expression of hate or abhorrence.
cataplexis: a threat of punishment, misfortune, or disaster.
compliment: performance of affected ceremonies.
comprobatio: complimenting one's judges or hearers.
deesis: vehement supplication of gods or men.
dehortatio: dissuasion, advice to the contrary.
diabole: prediction or denunciation of future events.
diasyrmus: disparagement of opponent's arguments.
dicaeologia: excusing by necessity.
donysis: describing or reenacting strong emotion.
ecphonesis: an exclamation expressing emotion.
emphasis: stress of language in such a way as to imply more than is actually stated.

encomium: praise of a person or thing by extolling inherent qualities.

epiplexis: asking a question in order to reproach.

erotesis: rhetorical question implying strong affirmation or denial.

eucharistia: giving thanks.

euche: vow or oath to keep a promise.

eulogia: commending or blessing a person or thing.

eustathia: pledge of constancy.

exordium: introduction; catching the interest of the audience.

exuscitatio: emotional utterance that moves hearers to like feelings.

hypocrisis: mocking an opponent through exaggeration of his gestures or speech habits.

indignatio: impassioned speech or loud, angry speaking.

inter se pugnantia: pointing out hypocrisy or inconsistency to opponent's face.

mempsis: complaining against injuries and pleading for help.

mycterismus: mockery of an opponent, accompanied by gestures.

oictros: evoking pity or forgiveness.

ominatio: a prophecy of evil.

onedismus: reproaching someone as ungrateful or impious.

optatio: a wish exclaimed.

orcos: an oath.

paeanismus: an exclamation of joy.

paramythia: consoling one who grieves.

pathopoeia: a general term for arousing passion or emotion.

peroration: an impassioned summary.

philophronesis: attempt to mitigate anger by gentle speech and humble submission.

proclees: vehement challenge to action.

protrope: exhorting hearers to action by threats and promises.

sarcasmus: a bitter gibe or taunt.

syngnome: forgiveness of injuries.

tapinosis: undignified language that debases a person or thing.

thaumasmus: exclamation of wonder.

threnos: lamentation.

3.8. Example, Allusion, and Citation of Authority

aenos: quoting wise sayings from fables.

analogy: reasoning or arguing from parallel cases.

anamnesis: recalling matters of the past.

antinomy: a comparison of one law, or part of a law, to another.
apodixis: referring to generally accepted principles or experience for confirmation.
apomnemonysis: quotation of an approved authority.
chria:
  a. a short exposition of a deed or saying of a person whose name is mentioned.
  b. a short rhetorical exercise that develops and varies a moral observation.
diatyposis: recommending useful precepts to someone else.
epicrisis: evaluating a quoted passage and commenting on it.
exemplum: an example cited, either true or feigned; illustrative story.
fable: a short, allegorical story.
homoeosis: general figure of similitude including icon, fable, paradigma, parable.
martyria: confirming something by one's own experience.
oraculum: quoting God's commandments.
parable: teaching a moral by means of an extended metaphor.
paroemia: quoting proverbs.
proverb: a short, pithy statement of a general truth. Category includes aphorism, gnome, maxim, adage, sententia.

3.9. Metaphorical Substitutions and Puns
agnominatio: repetition of a word with change in letter or sound.
allegory: an extended metaphor.
antanaclasis: homonymic pun.
antapodosis: a simile in which the objects compared correspond in several respects.
antonomasia: descriptive phrase for proper name or proper name for quality associated with it.
asteismus: facetious or mocking answer that plays on a word.
cacemphaton: scurrilous jest; lewd allusion or "double entendre."
catachresis: implied metaphor; extravagant, farfetched metaphor.
distinctio: specific reference to various meanings of a word.
euphemismus: circumlocution to palliate something unpleasant.
hyperbole: exaggerated or extravagant terms.
irony: expressing a meaning directly opposite the one intended.
meiosis: belittling, often through a trope of one word.
metalepsis: present effect attributed to a remote cause.

metonymy: substitution of cause for effect, effect for cause, proper name for one of its qualities, or vice versa.
parable: teaching a moral by means of an extended meatphor.
paronomasia: punning; playing on sound or meaning of words.
simile: explicit comparison.
synecdoche: substitution of part for whole, genus for species, or vice versa.

3.10. Repetitive Patterns

3.10.1. Repetition of letters, syllables, and sounds

alliteration: recurrence of an initial consonant sound, and sometimes of a vowel sound.
assonance: resemblance of proximal vowel sounds.
parechesis: repetition of the same sound in words in close succession.
parimion: a resolute alliteration in which every word in a sentence or phrase begins with the same letter.

3.10.2. Repetition of words

adjunctio: use of one verb to express similar ideas at the beginning or end of successive clauses.
agnominatio: repetition of a word with change in letter or sound.
anadiplosis: repetition of the last word of one line or clause to begin the next.
anaphora: repetition of the same word at the beginning of successive clauses or verses.
antistasis: repetition of a word in a different or contrary sense.
antistrophe: repetition of a closing word or words at the end of several successive clauses, sentences, or verses.
auxesis: words or clauses placed in climactic order.
catacosmesis: ordering words from greatest to least in dignity.
conduplicatio: repetition of a word or words in succeeding clauses.
diacope: repetition of a word with one or a few words in between.
diaphora: repetition of a common word rather than a proper name to signify qualities of the person as well as naming him.
epanalepsis: repetition at the end of a clause or sentence of the word with which it began.
epanaphora: intensive anaphora, *q.v.*

epistrophe: repetition of a closing word or words at the end of several clauses, sentences, or verses.

epizeuxis: repetition of a word with no other word in between.

homoioptoton: using various words with similar case endings in a sentence or line.

homoioteleuton: using various uninflected words with similar endings in a sentence or line.

hypozeuxis: every clause in a sentence has its own subject and verb.

ploce: repetition of a word with a new signification after the intervention of another word or words.

polyptoton: repetition of words from the same root but with different endings.

polysyndeton: use of a conjunction between each clause.

scesis onomaton: using a string of synonymous expressions.

symploce: a combination of anaphora and epistrophe, *q.v.*

3.10.3. Repetition of clauses, phrases, and ideas

auxesis: words or clauses placed in climactic order.

commoratio: emphasizing a strong point by repeating it several times in different words.

epimone: refrain; frequent repetition of a phrase or question.

epistrophe: repetition of a word or phrase at the end of several clauses, sentences, or verses.

exergasia: repeating the same thought in many figures.

homiologia: tedious, redundant style.

isocolon: repetition of phrases of equal length and usually corresponding structure.

pleonasmus: needless repetition of what has already been said or understood.

pysma: asking many questions that require diverse answers.

tautologia: repetition of the same idea in different words.

3.11. Techniques of Argument

alloiosis: breaking down a subject into alternatives.

amphidiorthosis: to hedge a charge made in anger by qualification.

anacoenosis: asking the opinion of one's hearers or readers.

analogy: reasoning or arguing from parallel cases.

antanagoge: balancing an unfavorable aspect with a favorable one.

anthypophora: asking questions and answering them.

antirrhesis: rejecting an argument because of its insignificance, error, or wickedness.

apodioxis: rejecting an argument indignantly as impertinent or absurdly false.

apomnemonysis: quotation of an approved authority.

apophasis:

    a. all alternatives rejected except one.

    b. pretending to ignore what is really affirmed.

    c. giving many reasons and confuting each one.

apoplanesis: evading the issue by digressing.

aporia: true or feigned doubt or deliberation about an issue.

aposiopesis: stopping suddenly in midcourse, leaving a statement unfinished.

argumentum ex concessis: reasoning from the premises of one's opponent.

comprobatio: complimenting one's judges or hearers.

concessio: conceding a point either to hurt an adversary or to prepare for a more important argument.

contrarium: one of two opposite statements is used to prove the other.

correctio:

    a. correcting a word or phrase used previously.

    b. preparing the audience to hear something unpleasant.

deliberatio: evaluating possible courses of action.

diaeresis: dividing genus into species in order to amplify.

dialogismus: speaking in another man's person.

dialysis: arguing from a series of disjunctive propositions.

diasyrmus: disparagement of opponent's arguments.

dicaeologia: excusing by necessity.

digestion: an orderly enumeration of points to be discussed.

dilemma: argument that offers an opponent only unacceptable choices.

emphasis: stress of language in such a way as to imply more than is actually stated.

enumeratio: a recapitulation.

epitrochasmus: a swift movement from one statement to another.

epitrope: ironical or earnest permission to an opponent or disputant.

erotesis: rhetorical question implying strong affirmation or denial.

euphemismus: circumlocution to palliate something unpleasant.

expeditio: rejection of all but one of various alternatives.

exuscitatio: emotional utterance that moves hearers to a like feeling.

heterogenium: irrelevant answer to distract attention.

hypophora: asking questions and answering them.

koinonia: consulting with one's opponents or with the judges.

leptologia: subtle speaking, quibbling.

medela: apology for the undeniable offenses of a friend.

metanoia: qualifying a statement by recalling it and expressing it in a different way.

metastasis:

   a. passing over an issue quickly.

   b. turning back an insult or objection against the person who made it.

oraculum: quoting God's commandments.

paradiegesis: using an observation of fact as a point of departure for a further, related observation.

paramologia: conceding a point either from conviction or to strengthen one's own argument.

parrhesia: candid speech.

periphrasis: circumlocution.

peristrophe: converting an opponent's argument to one's own use.

peroration: an impassioned summary.

philophronesis: trying to mitigate anger by gentle speech and humble submission.

procatalepsis: anticipating an objection and preventing it.

procatasceue: preparing an audience to tell them something one has done.

proecthesis: defending one's acts or statements.

progressio: advancing by steps of comparison.

prolepsis: applying now an attribute or epithet that will have relevancy later.

prosapodosis: supporting each alternative with a reason.

pseudomenos: an argument that forces one's adversary to lie.

ratiocinatio: a question addressed by the speaker to himself.

reditus ad propositum: return to the subject after a digression.

restrictio: excepting part of a statement already made.

sermocinatio: the speaker answers the remarks or questions of a pretended interlocuter.

significatio: to imply more than one says.

subjectio: the questioner suggests the answer to his own question.

syllogismus: intimation; hinting at something.

synchoresis: the speaker gives his questioners leave to judge him.

3.12. Ungrammatical, Illogical, or Unusual Uses of Language

acyrologia: use of an inexact or illogical word; malapropism.

amphibologia: ambivalence of grammatical structure, usually by mispunctuation.

anacoluthon: ending a sentence with a different structure from that with which it began.

anastrophe: unusual arrangement of words or clauses within a sentence.

anoiconometon: improper arrangement of words.

anthimeria: functional shift, using one part of speech for another.

anthypallage: change of grammatical case for emphasis.

antimetabole: inverting the order of repeated words.

antiphrasis: irony of one word, calling a "dwarf" a "giant."

antiptosis: substituting one case for another.

aschematiston: unskillful use of figures.

barbarismus: unnatural word-coinage or mispronunciation.

cacosyntheton: awkward transposition of the parts of a sentence.

cacozelia: affected diction made up of adaptation of Latin words; inkhorn terms.

catachresis: implied metaphor, using words wrenched from common usage.

enallage: substitution of one case, person, gender, number, tense, mood, part of speech, for another.

figure: a general term for any striking or unusual configuration of words or phrases.

graecismus: use of Greek idiom.

hebraism: use of Hebrew idiom.

hendyadis: expression of an idea by two nouns connected by "and" instead of a noun and its qualifier.

hypallage: awkward or humorous changing of agreement or application of words.

hyperbaton: a generic figure of various forms of departure from ordinary word order.

hysterologia: a phrase is interposed between a preposition and its object.

hysteron proteron: syntax out of normal logical or temporal order.

malapropism: a form of cacozelia; vulgar error through an attempt to seem learned.

metaplasm: moving letters or syllables of a word from their place; a generic term.

metathesis: type of metaplasm; transposition of letters out of normal order in a word.

poiciologia: awkward, ungrammatical speech.

solecismus: ignorant misuse of cases, genders, and tenses.

soriasmus: mingling of languages ignorantly or affectedly.

syllepsis: one verb lacking congruence with at least one subject that it governs.

synchisis: the word order of a sentence is confused.

4.

TERMS CLASSIFIED AS ORNAMENTS

The lists that follow are based on the summary of Geoffrey of Vinsauf (with reference to the *Rhetorica ad Herennium*) included as an appendix in Atkin's *English Literary Criticism: The Medieval Phase*. I have amplified a few definitions and changed that of "diminutio," since it seemed clear that Geoffrey of Vinsauf (Faral, p. 235, ll. 1236–1237, and p. 236, ll. 1285–1287) was following the usual meaning rather than inventing a new one.

4.1. Difficult Ornaments: Ten basic tropes
1. **onomatopoeia:** use of words that sound like their meanings.
2. **antonomasia:** descriptive phrase for proper name or proper name for quality associated with it.
3. **metonymy:** substitution of cause for effect or effect for cause; proper name for one of its qualities or vice versa.
4. **periphrasis:** circumlocution.
5. **hyperbaton:** generic figure for various forms of departure from ordinary word order.
6. **hyperbole:** exaggerated or extravagant terms used for emphasis.
7. **synecdoche:** substitution of part for whole, genus for species, or vice versa.
8. **catachresis:** implied metaphor.
9. **metaphor:** changing a word from its literal meaning to one analogous to it; assertion of identity.
10. **antimetabole:** inverting the order of repeated words.

4.2. Easy Ornaments

4.2.1. Figures of words
anaphora: repetition of same word at beginning of successive clauses or verses.

130

antistrophe: repetition of closing word or words at the end of several successive clauses or verses.

symploce: repetition of one word or phrase at the beginning, and another at the end, of successive clauses, sentences, or phrases.

ploce: repetition of word with new significance

conduplicatio: repetition of a word or words in succeeding clauses for amplification or to express emotion.

polyptoton: repetition of words from the same root but with different endings.

climax: mounting by degrees through words or sentences of increasing weight and in parallel construction.

interpretatione: repetition of an idea in different words.

antistasis: repetition of words in different or contrary senses.

contrarium: one of two opposite statements is used to prove the other.

compar: balancing of two clauses of equal length.

commutatio: order of first clause reversed in second.

homoioptoton: using various words with similar case endings in a sentence or line.

homoioteleuton: using various uninflected words with similar endings in a sentence or line.

asyndeton: omission of conjunctions between words, phrases, clauses.

articulo: succession of words without conjunctions.

continuatio: a continual heaping up of words; a long, full sentence.

aposiopesis: stopping suddenly in midcourse and leaving a statement unfinished.

metabasis: a brief statement of what has been said and what will follow.

conclusio: a brief summary.

erotesis: rhetorical question implying strong affirmation or denial.

ratiocinatio: a question addressed by the speaker to himself.

subjectio: the questioner suggests the answer to his own question.

horismus: a brief definition, often antithetical.

ecphonesis: exclamation expressing emotion.

sententia: a short, pithy statement of a general truth.

correctio: correction of a word or phrase used previously.

occupatio: a speaker emphasizes something by pointedly seeming to pass over it.

disjunctio: use of different verbs to express similar ideas in successive clauses.

conjunctio: clauses or phrases expressing similar ideas are held together by placing the verb between them.

adjunctio: use of one verb to express similar ideas at the beginning or end of successive clauses.

concessio: a speaker concedes a point either to hurt the adversary directly or in preparation for a more important argument.

aporia: true or feigned doubt or deliberation about an issue.

expeditio: rejection of all but one of various alternatives.

4.2.2. Figures of thought

parrhesia: candid speech; begging pardon in advance for necessary candor.

diminutio: litotes.

energia: clear, lucid, vivid description.

divisio:
- *a.* division into kinds or classes.
- *b.* dilemma.

accumulatio: heaping up praise or accusation.

exergasia: repeating the same thought in many figures.

commoratio: emphasizing a strong point by repeating it several times in different words.

antithesis: conjoining contrasting ideas.

simile: one thing is likened to another, dissimilar thing by the use of *like*, *as*, etc.

exemplum: an example cited, either true or feigned; illustrative story.

image: a thing that represents, or is taken to represent, something else; a symbol, emblem, representation.

effictio: personal description (outward appearance).

ethopoeia: personal description (character).

sermocinatio: the speaker answers his own remarks or questions.

prosopopoeia: an imaginary or absent person is represented as speaking or acting.

significatio: to imply more than one says; innuendo.

brevitas: concise expression.

demonstratio: vivid description.

distribution: dividing the whole into its parts.

5.

TERMS ESPECIALLY USEFUL IN LITERARY CRITICISM

The list that follows contains sometimes shortened repetitions of some of the definitions listed in chapter 1. For full definitions and cross-references, see the main listing in chapter 1.

Allegory. See entry, chapter 1.

Alliteration. Originally, recurrence of an initial consonant sound, but now sometimes used of vowel sounds as well, where it overlaps with **Assonance,** *q.v.*:

> "Warm-laid grave of a womb-life grey;
> Manger, maiden's knee. . . ."
> (G. M. Hopkins)

Amplification. Rhetorical device used to expand a simple statement; one sixteenth-century English theorist isolated five means of amplification (comparison, division, accumulation, intimation, progression) and the following figures that amplify: **Hyperbole; Correctio; Paralepsis; Accumulatio; Divisio; Interrogatio; Exclamatio; Synoeciosis; Antithesis; Sententia.** Another theorist lists seventeen figures, a third sixty-four; logically, *any* figure except those specifically aimed at brevity should fit.

Anacoluthon (a na co LU thon; G. "inconsistent, anomalous") —
Anantapodoton. Ending a sentence with a different structure from that with which it began. Both a vice and a device to demonstrate emotion:

> "Rather proclaim it, Westmoreland, through my host,
> That he which hath no stomach to this fight,
> Let him depart."
> (*Henry V*, IV, iii)

Anadiplosis (a na di PLO sis; G. "doubled back") — **Gradatio; Palilogia (1); Reduplicatio; Duplicatio; Redouble.** *See also* **Con-**

duplicatio. Repetition of the last word of one line or clause to begin the next:

> "For I have loved long, I crave reward
> Reward me not unkindly: think on kindness,
> Kindness becommeth those of high regard
> Regard with clemency a poor man's blindness. . . ."
> (Bartholomew Griffin, *Fidessa*, XVI)

Anaphora (a NAPH o ra; G. "carrying back") — **Repetitio; Iteratio; Epanaphora; Epembasis; Report.** Repetition of the same word at the beginning of successive clauses or verses:

> "To think on death it is a misery, To think on life it is
> a vanity; To think on the world verily it is, To think that
> here man hath no perfect bliss."
> (Puttenham)

Anastrophe (a NAS tro phe; G. "turning back") — **Reversio.** *See also* **Hysteron Proteron.** Kind of **Hyperbaton:** unusual arrangement of words or clauses within a sentence.

> "Yet I'll not shed her blood;
> Nor scar that whiter skin of hers than snow."
> (*Othello*, V, ii)

Anatomy (G. "cutting up, dissection"). The analysis of an issue into its constituent parts, for ease of discussion or clarity of exegesis; the term is not a traditional one, but has been increasingly used as a generic term for a technique that includes a number of the traditional dividing and particularizing figures.

Antanaclasis (an tan AC la sis; G. "reflection, bending back") — **Transplacement; Anaclasis; Rebounde; Reciprocatio; Refractio.**

1. Homonymic pun: "My forces razde, thy banners raisd within" (Sidney, *Astrophil and Stella*, XXXVI).
2. Sometimes **Ploce.**

Antimetabole (an ti me TAB o le; G. "turning about") — **Chiasmus; Commutatio; Permutatio; Counterchange.** Inverting the order of repeated words to sharpen their sense or contrast the ideas they convey or both; chiasmus and commutatio sometimes imply a more precise balance and reversal, antimetabole a looser, but they are virtual synonyms: "I pretty, and my saying apt? or I apt, and my saying pretty?" (*Love's Labour's Lost*, I, ii).

Antistrophe (an TIS tro phe; G. "turning about").

1. **Conversio; Conversum; Counterturne; Epiphora; Epistro-**

phe (1). Repetition of a closing word or words at the end of several successive clauses, sentences, or verses:
"Where affections bear rule, there reason is subdued, honesty is subdued, good will is subdued, and all things else that withstand evil, for ever are subdued" (Wilson).

2. The repetition of a word or phrase in a second context in the same position it held in an earlier and similar context:
". . . anon with great disdain,
She shuns my love, and after by a train
She seeks my love, and saith she loves me most,
But seeing her love, so lightly won and lost." etc.
(Peacham)

Antithesis (an TITH e sis; G. "opposition") — **Antitheton; Contentio; Contraposition; Oppositio.** *See also* **Synchisis.** Conjoining contrasting ideas, as in Sidney's *Arcadia*:
". . . neither the one hurt her, nor the other help her;
just without partiality, mighty without contradiction,
liberal without losing, wise without curiosity. . . ."

Antonomasia (an ton o MA si a; G. "to name instead," "to use an epithet, patronymic, instead of a proper name") — **Pronominatio; Nominatio; Surnamer.** Descriptive phrase for proper name or proper name for quality associated with it:
"If someone speaking of the Gracchi should say: 'Surely the grandsons of Africanus did not behave like this.' "
(*Rhetorica ad Herennium*, IV, xxxi, 42)

Aposiopesis (ap o si o PE sis; G. "becoming silent") — **Praecisio; Reticentia; Obticentia; Silence; Interruption.**

1. Stopping suddenly in midcourse — leaving a statement unfinished:
"He said you were, I dare not tell you plain:
For words once out, never return again."
(Puttenham)

2. An idea, though unexpressed, is clearly perceived, as when Sir Winston Churchill is said to have replied to an impertinent question: "The answer to your question, sir, is in the plural, and they bounce."

Apostrophe (G. "turning away") — **Aversio; Turne Tale.** Break-

ing off discourse to address directly some person or thing either
present or absent:

"Soul of the age!
The applause, delight, the wonder of our stage!
My Shakespeare rise!"

(Ben Jonson)

Assonance (L. "to sound to"). Resemblance or similarity in
sound between vowel-sounds preceded and followed by differing
consonant-sounds in words in proximity: will; hinder; nit. *See
also* **Alliteration; Paronomasia.**

Asyndeton (a SYN de ton; G. "unconnected") — **Brachylogia;
Dialyton** (1); **Dissolutio; Loose Language; Dialelumenon.** Omission of conjunctions between words, phrases, or clauses:

"Faynt, wearie, sore, emboyled, grieved, brent
With heat, toyle, wounds, armes, smart, and inward fire."

(Spenser, *Faerie Queene*, I, xi, 28)

Opposite of **Polysyndeton.**

Catachresis (cat a CHRE sis; G. "misuse, misapplication") —
Abuse.

1. Implied metaphor, using words wrenched from common
   usage, as when Hamlet says, "I will speak daggers to her."
2. A second definition that seems slightly different but perhaps
   is not: an extravagant, unexpected, farfetched metaphor,
   as when a weeping woman's eyes become Niagara Falls.

Chiasmus (chi AS mus; G. "crossing") — **Antimetabole; Commutatio.** The term is derived from the Greek letter X (chi),
whose shape, if the two halves of the construction are rendered
in separate verses, it resembles:

"Polish'd in courts, and harden'd in the field,
Renown'd for conquest, and in council skill'd."

(Addison, "The Campaign")

Climax (G. "ladder") — **Gradatio; Ascendus; Methalemsis;
Marching Figure.** Mounting by degrees through words or sentences of increasing weight and in parallel construction: "Labour
getteth learning, learning getteth fame, fame getteth honour, honour getteth bliss forever" (Wilson).

See also **Auxesis; Anadiplosis.**

Diabole (di A bo le; G. "false accusation, slander," from "to throw across"). A prediction of (and sometimes a denunciation of) things that are to take place in the future:

> "Then he took unto him the twelve, and said unto them, Behold, we go up to Jerusalem, and all things that are written by the prophets concerning the Son of man shall be accomplished. For he shall be delivered unto the Gentiles, and shall be mocked, and spitefully entreated, and spitted on: And they shall scourge him, and put him to death: and the third day he shall rise again."
>
> (Luke 18:31–33)

Diacope (di A co pe; G. "cleft, gash").

1. **Tmesis.** Repetition of a word with one or a few words in between: "My heart is fixed, O God, my heart is fixed" (Peacham).
2. **Dieremenon; Disparsum.** Separation of the elements of a compound word by another word or words: "West — by God — Virginia."

Effictio (ef FIC ti o; L. "fashioning"). Personal description (outward appearance); the head-to-toe itemization of a heroine's charms, common in earlier English poetry:

> "My Lady's hair is threads of beaten gold,
>   Her front the purest Chrystal eye hath seen:
> Her eyes the brightest stars the heavens hold,
>   Her cheeks red roses such as seld have been:
> Her pretty lips of red vermillion dye,
>   Her hands of ivory the purest white:
> Her blush Aurora, or the morning sky,
>   Her breast displays two silver fountains bright,
> The Spheres her voice, her grace the Graces three,
>   Her body is the Saint that I adore,
> Her smiles and favors sweet as honey be,
>   Her feet fair Thetis praiseth evermore.
> But ah the worst and last is yet behind,
> For of a Gryphon she doth bear the mind."
>
> (Griffin, *Fidessa*, XXXIX)

Ellipsis (el LIP sis; G. "to fall short; leave out"); alt. sp. **Eclipsis — Brachylogia; Default.** *See also* **Praegnans Constructio.**

Omission of a word easily understood: "And he to England shall along with you" (*Hamlet*, III, iii).

Encomium (G. "eulogy"); alt. sp. **Ecomium — Commendatio.** Praise of a person or thing by extolling inherent qualities. *See also* **Comprobatio; Eulogia.**

Energia (en er GI a; G. "activity"; rhet. "vigor of style") — **Hypotyposis; Descriptio; Informatio; Diatyposis** (1).

1. Clear, lucid, vivid description.
2. Generic term that includes: **Ethopoeia; Characterismus; Prosopographia; Prosopopoeia; Mimesis; Dialogismus; Pragmatographia; Topographia; Topothesia; Icon; Pathopoeia; Sermocinatio.** *See also* **Enargia.**

Enumeratio (e num er A ti o). Division of subject into adjuncts, cause into effects, antecedent into consequents. *See also* **Digestion; Eutrepismus:**

"How do I love thee? Let me count the ways.
I love thee to the depth and breadth and height
My soul can reach, when feeling out of sight
For the ends of Being and ideal Grace.
I love thee to the level of everyday's
Most quiet need, by sun and candlelight.
I love thee freely, as men strive for Right;
I love thee purely, as they turn from Praise.
I love thee with the passion put to use
In my old griefs, and with my childhood's faith.
I love thee with a love I seemed to lose
With my lost saints, — I love thee with the breath,
Smiles, tears, of all my life! — and, if God choose,
I shall but love thee better after death."

(Elizabeth Barrett Browning)

Epanalepsis (ep a na LEP sis; G. "resumption, repetition") — **Epanadiplosis; Repetitio; Slowe Returne; Eccho Sounde.** Repetition at the end of a clause or sentence of the word with which it began: "I might, unhappy word, O me, I might" (Sidney, *Astrophil and Stella*, XXXIII).

Epistrophe (e PIS tro phe; G. "turning away").

1. Rhet. **Antistrophe** (1); **Epiphora.** Repetition of a closing word or words at the end of several clauses, sentences, or verses: "And all the night he did nothing but weep Philoclea, sigh Philoclea, and cry out Philoclea" (Sidney, *New Arcadia*, III).

TERMS USEFUL IN LITERARY CRITICISM 139

2. Log.: conversion of a proposition.

Epizeuxis (ep i ZEUX is; G. "fastening upon") — **Doublet; Geminatio; Cuckowspell; Underlay.** Emphatic repetition of a word with no other words between: "O horror, horror, horror!" *See also* **Palilogia** (2).

Euphuism. See main entry, chapter 1.

Exemplum (ex EM plum; L. "a sample") — **Paradigma.** An example cited, either true or feigned; illustrative story. *See also* **Paradiegesis.**

"Such first was *Bacchus*, that with furious might
All th'East before vntam'd did ouerronne,
And wrong repressed, and establisht right,
Which lawlesse men had formerly fordonne.
There Iustice first her princely rule begonne.
Next *Hercules* his like ensample shewed,
Who all the West with equall conquest wonne,
And monstrous tyrants with his club subdewed;
The club of Iustice dread, with kingly powre endewed."
(Spenser, *Faerie Queene*, V, i, 2)

Hendyadis (hen DY a dis; G. "one by means of two"); alt. sp. **Hendyasis** — **Twinnes.** Expression of an idea by two nouns connected by "and" instead of a noun and its qualifier: "by length of time and siege" for "by a long siege." Peacham, ignoring the derivation of the term, defines it as the substituting, for an adjective, of a substantive with the same meaning: "a man of great wisdom" for "a wise man." This redefinition would make it a kind of **Anthimeria,** *q.v.*

Homoioptoton. See main entry, chapter 1.

Homoioteleuton. See main entry, chapter 1.

Hyperbaton. See main entry, chapter 1.

Hyperbole (hy PER bo le; G. "excess, exaggeration") — **Superlatio; Loud Lyer; Overreacher.** Exaggerated or extravagant terms used for emphasis and not intended to be understood literally; self-conscious exaggeration:

"For instance, of a Lion;
He roared so loud, and looked so wondrous grim,
His very shadow durst not follow him."
(Pope, *Peri Bathous*)

Hypotaxis (hy po TAX is; G. "subjection"). An arrangement of clauses or phrases in a dependent or subordinate relationship. Opposite of **Parataxis.**

"Antiquity held too light thoughts from objects of mortality, while some drew provocatives of mirth from anatomies, and jugglers showed tricks with skeletons, when fiddlers made not so pleasent mirth as fencers, and men could sit with quiet stomachs while hanging was played before them."
                (Sir Thomas Browne, *Hydriotaphia*, chap. 3)
Hysteron Proteron (HYS te ron   PRO te ron; G. "the latter [put as] the former") — **Preposterous.** Form of **Hyperbaton:** syntax out of normal logical or temporal order:
"ENOBARBUS: Th'Antoniad, the Egyptian admiral,
                With all their sixty, fly and turn the rudder."
                (*Antony and Cleopatra*, III, x)
See also **Anastrophe.**
Irony. See main entry, chapter 1.
Isocolon (i SO COL on; G. "of equal members or clauses") — **Compar; Parison; Parimembre; Even.**
   1. Repetition of phrases of equal length and usually corresponding structure.
      a. **Compar:** balancing of two clauses of equal length.
      b. **Parison:** long phrases or clauses in parallel construction sometimes with similar sounds in similar places in the parallel phrases or clauses: Nathaniel to Holofernes: "Your reasons at dinner have been sharp and sententious; pleasant without scurrility, witty without affection, audacious without impudency, learned without opinion, and strange without heresy" (*Love's Labour's Lost*, V, i).
   2. G. rhet.: two or more clauses with the same number of syllables.
Litotes (LI to tes; G. "plainness, simplicity") — **Diminutio; Exadversio; Moderatour; Tenuitas.** Denial of the contrary; opposite of amplification; understatement that intensifies: "he likes his wife not a little" for "he dotes on her." *See also* **Extenuatio.**
Malapropism. A form of **Cacozelia;** vulgar error through an attempt to seem learned; not, properly speaking, a rhetorical term. The word comes from Mrs. Malaprop, a character in Sheridan's *The Rivals* (1775). Also sometimes means **Acyrologia.**
"MRS. MALAPROP: Now don't attempt to extirpate yourself from the matter: you know I have proof controvertible of it."
Meiosis (mei o sis; G. "lessening") — **Imminutio; Disabler.** To

belittle, often through a trope of one word; use a degrading epithet: "childish carriage" for "Rolls Royce." *See also* **Litotes.**
Metaphor. See main entry, chapter 1.
Metaplasm (MET a plasm; G. "to mold into a new form"). Moving from their natural place the letters or syllables of a word. Generic term. *See* **Prothesis; Aphaeresis; Epenthesis; Syncope; Paragoge; Apocope; Systole; Diastole; Ellipsis; Synaloepha; Synaeresis; Diaeresis; Antisthecon; Metathesis.**
Metonymy (me TON y my; G. "change of name") — **Denominatio; Transnominatio; Transmutation; Misnamer.** There are four types corresponding to the four **Causes,** *q.v.* Substitution of cause for effect or effect for cause, proper name for one of its qualities or vice versa; so the Wife of Bath is spoken of as half Venus and half Mars to denote her unique mixture of love and strife.
Occupatio (oc cu PA ti o) — **Occultatio; Praeteritio; Paralepsis; Parasiopesis.** A speaker emphasizes something by pointedly seeming to pass over it, as in introducing a guest speaker one says, "I will not dwell here on the twenty books and the thirty articles Professor X has written, nor his forty years as Dean, nor his many illustrious pupils, but only say . . . ."
Onomatopoeia (on o mat o poe I a; G. "the making of words") **Nominatio; Procreatio; Nominis Fictio; Newnamer.** Use or invention of words that sound like their meaning: "the murmur of innumerable bees"; "riff-raff."
Oxymoron (OX y MOR on; G. "a witty, paradoxical saying"). A condensed paradox; Milton's "darkness visible," for example.
Paradox (G. "contrary to opinion or expectation") — **Wonderer.** A seemingly self-contradictory statement, which yet is shown to be (sometimes in a surprising way) true: "She makes the black night bright by smiling on it."
Parataxis (para TAX is; G. "placing side by side"). Clauses or phrases arranged independently (a coordinate, rather than a subordinate, construction), sometimes, as here, without the customary connectives: "I came, I saw, I conquered." Opposite of **Hypotaxis.**
Paroemia (pa ROEM i a; G. "byword, proverb").
   1. **Adage; Proverb; Apothegm; Sententia; Maxim; Aphorismus; Gnome.**
   2. Quoting proverbs: as a further source of confusion, the terms in the first definition are sometimes used to mean *quoting* proverbs as well as the proverbs themselves.

Paronomasia (par on o MAS i a) — **Adnominatio,** *q.v.*; **Adfictio; Skesis.** Punning; playing on the sounds and meaning of words; unlike **Antanaclasis** in that the words punned on are similar but not identical in sound. Falstaff includes both kinds in jesting with Prince Hal: "Were it not here apparent that thou art heir apparent . . ." (*I Henry IV*, I, ii).

Period. See main entry, chapter 1.

Periphrasis (pe RIPH ra sis; G. "circumlocution") — **Circuitio; Ambage.** Circumlocution.

Pleonasmus (ple on AS mus; G. "excess") — **Macrologia; Too Full Speech.** Needless repetition: "I spoke the words with my own mouth."

Ploce (PLO ce; G. "plaiting") — **Traductio; Copulatio; Conexio; Diaphora; Swift Repeate.** Repetition of a word with a new signification after the intervention of another word or words. Peacham would confine this term to repetition of a proper name, specifying diaphora for repetition of ordinary words:

> "He whilest he liued, happie was through thee,
> And being dead is happie now much more;
> Liuing, that lincked chaunst with thee to bee,
> And dead, because him dead thou dost adore
> As liuing, and thy lost deare loue deplore."
>   (Spenser, *The Rvines of Time*)

See also **Epanodos** (2); **Epiploce.**

Polyptoton (po lyp TO ton; G. "employment of the same word in various cases"); alt. sp. **Polyptiton** — **Paregmenon; Adnominatio; Traductio** (2); **Multiclinatum.** Repetition of words from the same root but with different endings: "Society is no comfort to one not sociable."

Polysyndeton (poly SYN de ton) — **Coople Clause.** Use of a conjunction between each clause; opposite of **Asyndeton:** Milton says of Satan, in his course through Chaos, that he

> "pursues his way,
> And swims, or sinks, or wades, or creeps, or flies."
>   (*Paradise Lost*, II, 950)

Prosopopoeia. See main entry, chapter 1.

Senecan Style. See main entry, chapter 1.

Simile (L. "like") — **Similitude.** One thing is likened to another, dissimilar thing by the use of *like, as,* etc.; distinguished from **Metaphor** in that the comparison is made explicit: "My love is like a red, red rose."

Syllepsis (syl LEP sis; G. "taking together") — **Double Supply.**
One verb lacking congruence with at least one subject that it
governs: "The Nobles and the King was taken." This device can
easily be used as a pun. It differs from zeugma in that zeugma
has no faulty congruence. *See* **Zeugma.**

Synalepha (syn a LEPH a; G. "to smear or melt together"); alt.
sp. **Synaloepha.**

1. First of two adjacent vowels is elided; "t'attain" for "to
   attain."
2. One of two adjacent vowels is elided; or rather, the two
   vowels are fused into one.

Synecdoche (sy NEC do che; G. "understanding one thing with
another") — **Intellectio; Quick Conceite.** Substitution of part
for whole, genus for species, or vice versa: "All hands on deck."

Tapinosis (tap i NO sis; G. "reduction; humiliation; lowness of
style") — **Humilatio; Abbaser.** Undignified language that debases a person or thing: "rhymester" for "poet," "verses" for
"poetry."

Tautologia (taut o LO gi a; G. "saying the same things") —
Pleonasmus; Circumlocution; Selfe Saying. Repetition of the
same idea in different words:

"LEPIDUS: What manner o'thing is your crocodile?

ANTONY: It is shap'd, sir, like itself, and it is as broad
        as it has breadth. It is just so high as it is, and
        moves with its own organs. It lives by that
        which nourisheth it, and the elements once
        out of it, it transmigrates.

LEPIDUS: What colour is it of?

ANTONY: Of its own colour too.

LEPIDUS: 'Tis a strange serpent.

ANTONY: 'Tis so. And the tears of it are wet."

                    (*Antony and Cleopatra*, II, vii)

Trope. See main entry, chapter 1.

Zeugma (ZEUG ma; G. "yoking") — **Single Supply; Synzeugmenon.** One verb governs several congruent words or clauses, each
in a different way, as in *The Rape of the Lock*:

"Here thou, great *Anna!* whom three realms obey,
    Dost sometimes counsel take — and sometimes Tea."

The term **Hyperzeugma** is sometimes used when every object in a
series has its own verb or preposition. *See* **Prozeugma; Mezozeugma; Hypozeugma; Epezeugmenon; Syllepsis.**

6.

SOME IMPORTANT DATES

ca. 483–376 B.C.	Gorgias
436–338	Isocrates
ca. 370 (?)	Plato, *Phaedrus*
ca. 357	Plato, *Gorgias*
ca. 330	Aristotle, *Rhetorica*
fl. ca. 150	Hermagoras
86–82	[Cicero], *Rhetorica ad Herennium*
84	Cicero, *De Inventione*
55	Cicero, *De Oratore*
46	Cicero, *Orator* and *Brutus*
44	Cicero, *Topica*
30–38	Dionysius of Halicarnassus, *On the Arrangement of Words; On the Ancient Orators*
95 A.D.	Quintilian, *Institutio Oratoria*
ca. 1st cent. (possibly 1st cent. B.C.)	[Demetrius], *On Style*
ca. 1st or 3d cent.	[Longinus], *On the Sublime*
ca. 700	Bede, *Liber de Schematibus et Tropis*
ca. 1200	Geoffrey of Vinsauf, *Poetria Nova; Summa de Coloribus Rhetoricis*
1524 (?)	Cox, Leonard, *The Arte or Crafte of Rhetoryke*
1540	Susenbrotus, Joannes, *Epitome troporum ac schematum et grammaticorum et rhetoricorum*
1544	Talaeus, Audomarus, *Institutiones Oratoriae*
1550	Sherry, Richard, *A Treatise of Schemes and Tropes*

144

1553	Wilson, Thomas, *The Arte of Rhetorique*
1555	Sherry, Richard, *A Treatise of the Figures of Grammar and Rhetorike*
	Ramus, Peter, *Dialectique*
1563	Rainolde, Richard, *A Booke Called the Foundacion of Rhetorike*
1576	Sturm, John, *De universa ratione elocutionis rhetoricae*
1577	Peacham, Henry, *The Garden of Eloquence*
1584	Fenner, Dudley, *The Arts of Logike and Rhetorike*
1588	Fraunce, Abraham, *The Arcadian Rhetorike*
1589	Puttenham, George, *The Arte of English Poesie*
1592	Day, Angel, *The English Secretorie*
1593	Peacham, Henry, *The Garden of Eloquence* (revised and enlarged)
1598	Butler, Charles, *Rhetoricae Libri Duo*
1599	Hoskyns, John, *Dirrecions for Speech and Style*
1657	Smith, John, *The Mysterie of Rhetorique Unvail'd*

7.

WORKS CITED

Classical Treatises

Aristotle. *Rhetorica*. Trans. W. Rhys Roberts. In *The Works of Aristotle*, vol. 9. Ed. W. D. Ross. Oxford, 1924.

Cicero. *De Inventione* and *Topica*. Trans. H. M. Hubbell. Loeb Classical Library, 1949.

————. *De Oratore*. Trans. E. W. Sutton and H. Rackham. Rev. ed. Loeb Classical Library, 1959. 2 vols.

————. *Orator*. Trans. H. M. Hubbell; *Brutus*. Trans. G. L. Hendrickson. Loeb Classical Library, 1939.

[Cicero]. *Ad C. Herennium: De Ratione Dicendi* (*Rhetorica ad Herennium*). Trans. Harry Caplan. Loeb Classical Library, 1954.

[Demetrius]. *On Style*. Trans. W. Rhys Roberts. Rev. ed. Loeb Classical Library, 1960.

Diogenes Laertius. *Lives of Eminent Philosophers*. Trans. R. D. Hicks. Loeb Classical Library, 1925. 2 vols.

Halm, Carolus. *Rhetores Latini Minores*. Leipzig, 1863.

Quintilian. *Institutio Oratoria*. Trans. H. E. Butler. Loeb Classical Library, 1920–1922. 4 vols.

Medieval and Renaissance Treatises

Butler, Charles. *Rhetoricae Libri Duo* [1598]. London, 1629.

Day, Angel. *The English Secretorie* [1592]. London, 1635.

Faral, Edmond. *Les Arts Poétiques du XIIe et du XIIIe Siècle*. Paris, 1924.

Fenner, Dudley. *The Artes of Logike and Rhetorike*. Middelburg, 1584.

Fraunce, Abraham. *The Arcadian Rhetorike*. Edited by Ethel Seaton from the 1588 ed. Oxford, 1950.

Hoskyns, John. "Direccions for Speech and Style" [*ca.* 1599]. Printed from MS Harley 4604. In *Life, Letters and Writings of John Hoskyns, 1566–1638*. Ed. Louise Brown Osborn. New Haven, 1937. Pp. 114–166.

Peacham, Henry. *The Garden of Eloquence*. London, 1577.

————. *The Garden of Eloquence (1593)*. Facsimile reproduction with introduction by William G. Crane. Gainesville, Florida, 1954.

Puttenham, George. *The Arte of English Poesie* [1589]. Ed. Gladys Doidge Willcock and Alice Walker. Cambridge, 1936.

Rainolde, Richard. *A Booke Called the Foundacion of Rhetorike*. London, 1563.

Sherry, Richard. *A Treatise of Schemes and Tropes* [1550]. Facsimile reproduction with introduction and index by Herbert W. Hildebrandt. Gainesville, Florida, 1961.

————. *A Treatise of the Figures of Grammar and Rhetorike*. London, 1555.

Smith, John. *The Mysterie of Rhetorique Unvail'd*. London, 1657.

Susenbrotus, Joannes. *Epitome troporum ac schematum et grammaticorum et rhetoricorum* [Zurich, 1540]. London, 1567.

Wilson, Thomas. *The Arte of Rhetorique* [1553]. Ed. G. H. Mair. Oxford, 1909.

Modern Treatises and Discussions

Atkins, J. W. H. *English Literary Criticism: The Medieval Phase*. New York, 1943.

Auerbach, Eric. *Literary Language and Its Public*. Trans. Ralph Manheim. London, 1965.

Barish, Jonas A. "The Prose Style of John Lyly," *ELH*, XXIII (March, 1956), 14–27.

————. "Baroque Prose in the Theater: Ben Jonson," *PMLA*, LXXIII (June, 1958).

Burke, Kenneth. *A Grammar of Motives*. New York, 1945.

————. *A Rhetoric of Motives*. New York, 1950.

Copi, Irving M. *Introduction to Logic*. 2d ed. New York, 1961.

Croll, Morris J. *Style, Rhetoric, and Rhythm*. Essays ed. J. Max Patrick, *et al*. Princeton, 1966.

Curtius, Ernst Robert. *European Literature and the Latin Middle Ages*. Bollingen Series, XXXVI. Trans. Willard R. Trask. New York, 1953.

Fletcher, Angus. *Allegory: The Theory of a Symbolic Mode*. Ithaca, 1964.

Frye, Northrop. *Anatomy of Criticism*. Princeton, 1957.

————. *The Well-Tempered Critic.* Bloomington, 1963.

Hough, Graham. *A Preface to the "Faerie Queene."* London, 1962.

Howell, Wilbur S. *Logic and Rhetoric in England, 1500–1700.* New York, 1961.

Hunter, G. K. *John Lyly: The Humanist as Courtier.* London, 1962.

Joseph, Sister Miriam, C.S.C. *Shakespeare's Use of the Arts of Language.* New York, 1947.

Kennedy, George. *The Art of Persuasion in Greece.* Princeton, 1963.

Ogden, C. K., and I. A. Richards. *The Meaning of Meaning.* 8th ed. New York, 1956.

Richards, I. A. *The Philosophy of Rhetoric.* Oxford, 1936.

Rix, Herbert David. *Rhetoric in Spenser's Poetry.* Pennsylvania State College Studies, no. 7. State College, Penna., 1940.

Rubel, Veré L. *Poetic Diction in the English Renaissance.* New York, 1941.

Smyth, Herbert Weir. *Greek Grammar.* Rev. by Gordon M. Messing. Cambridge, Mass., 1956.

Taylor, Warren. *Tudor Figures of Rhetoric.* [Chicago], 1937. Distributed by the University of Chicago libraries.

Tuve, Rosemond. *Elizabethan and Metaphysical Imagery.* Chicago, 1947.

Williamson, George. *The Senecan Amble.* London, 1951.